complete **home** makeover

Woman's Value

complete home makeover

Anneke Blaise, Karen Geldenhuys & Wilma Howells

Tafelberg

The publisher thanks **Old Mutual Bank**
for supporting the marketing of this book

A house is one of the most important purchases you will ever make so buying and renovating your home should be seen as part of your complete financial plan. It makes sense to discuss and finance your home makeover with a bank that takes into account your dreams, commitments, savings and investments. Old Mutual Bank, a division of Nedbank Ltd, has branches staffed with people who can help make your dream home a reality. You can visit an Old Mutual Bank branch, contact the Old Mutual Bank Client Call Centre on 0860 555 222 or access the website www.oldmutual.co.za. You can also contact your nearest Old Mutual personal financial adviser or broker for more information.

BANK

A division of Nedbank Ltd. Reg. No. 1951/000009/06.

First Published in 2004 by

Tafelberg

Tafelberg Publishers
Heerengracht 40, Cape Town 8000
Registration nr.: 51/02378/06
10 9 8 7 6 5 4 3 2 1

Publisher Anita Pyke
Editor Nicky Metz, Lizé Lübbe
Proofreaders Brenda Brickman, Barbara Mowatt,
    Tracey Greenwood
Design Odette Marais
Photography Neville Lockhart,
    Anél van der Merwe, Adriaan Oosthuizen
Index Brenda Brickman
Production Andrew de Kock

Cover photograph Neville Lockhart
Styling Anneke Blaise, Ilse de Klerk
Furniture and props Weylandts Home Store,
    Jenna Gifford (curtain)

Reproduction by Unifoto (Pty) Ltd, Cape Town
Printed and bound by
    Tien Wah Press (Pte) Ltd, Singapore
ISBN 0 624 04 1301

contents

B19

B19-1
Pale Melon

B19-4
Shallot

B19-6
New Home

D3

D3-1
Mauve Mist

D3-2
Shy Cream

D3-3
Mild May

introduction

Even in a creative work environment like ours, it is not often that a project comes along that is as exciting and stimulating as our **Woman's Value** House and this resulting book. And it does not matter that it was our creative team that initially put 'a house to play in and shoot in' on their annual wish list, when they were told to go out and find a house to revamp, the challenge was almost overwhelming.

What started as a wild idea turned out to suit just about everyone. Our creative team would get the blank canvas they wished for and it offered the perfect opportunity for our DIY and décor clients to become part of our medium in a practical, hands-on way. It also gave us a wonderful marketing tool that has had fantastic exposure on television and radio and has enticed readers to buy the magazine since this house is the best prize any reader of our magazine could have the chance to win. All in all, too good an opportunity to pass by. And so we didn't.

The perfect house turned out to be an old farmhouse in Mowbray. Over a period of nine months our readers had the opportunity to see the transformation room by room. With a mix of clever ideas, crafty makes and excellent products, we managed to add immense value to the house. Throughout this book you will see the continual references to 'our house', having been the starting point to our inspiration for this book.

before

At the office, the enormity of the task we set ourselves soon became very clear. For the best part of six months we saw very little of Anneke Blaise, our creative director and project manager for the **Woman's Value** House, and craft and décor editor Wilma Howells. Suddenly their main job was 'on site' directing builders and painters and workmen, to knock down walls, build new ones, move sockets, sand floors, lay tiles ... and plan the striking result you'll see in **Complete Home Makeover**.

One by one the rooms came to life – fresh, contemporary rooms with modern finishes but also with all the character of the original old farmhouse. Small touches added charm and value, and transformed it into a house one can live in comfortably. As the project progressed, we all became only too aware of the pluses and pitfalls of renovating, and the importance of proper planning. And, being a practical, how-to and ideas magazine, we simply could not resist sharing this experience with you.

If this book takes at least some of the pain out of the process and inspires you with a couple of really workable bright ideas, our job will have been well done. Thanks to all the sponsors that made it possible.

Happy renovating.

Terena

Editor, **Woman's Value/** *dit*

Buying a house is probably one of the biggest long-term investments you will ever make. Whether you're buying a house to sell at a profit or have just purchased your dream home, there are a myriad things you can do, and small improvements you can make that will add great value to your investment.

adding value

Home improvement should be done with careful consideration and care. In much the same way that the right changes and additions are going to add value to your home, or make your house more appealing to a prospective buyer, the wrong changes and additions will have the opposite effect.

You should, therefore, ensure that you are actually making improvements and not simply adding decorations that you personally like, but that will have very little appeal to anyone else.

You may choose to go the renovate-and-restore route, or (if you have a generous budget) to replace everything that is old and ring in the new. Whatever you decide to do, keep in mind that this house is going to be your (or a prospective buyer's) home for some time to come. Home improvements should add more than just monetary value to your investment. The changes you make should be good quality improvements that, in turn, will ensure good quality living – a gain more valuable than cash.

Simple improvements

When viewing a house, prospective buyers usually look for a few important basics. The following improvements and additions will increase the value and appeal of your house, and can easily turn it into a dream home:

◀ A modern kitchen. A kitchen can make or break the sale of a house. Make sure your kitchen is well laid out, has ample work surfaces and lots of storage space. Allow enough room for major appliances.

◀ A garage. A garage can increase the value of an urban property by up to 20 percent. If you have one, best not turn it into a living area. If you don't have a garage, have a look at your property plans and establish whether there is enough space to erect one. Keep in mind that you might need planning permission and building regulations approval.

◀ Update your bathrooms. An outdated bathroom can easily be transformed with a simple coat or two of paint. Colour plays an important role in the bathroom – choose the colour scheme wisely. A darkly painted bathroom might appear dingy, and won't appeal to any prospective buyers. A white suite is the safest option.

Mixer taps are always favoured, as is a separate bath and a free-standing shower. If you have room to add an en-suite bathroom, do so. The ideal is to have an extra bathroom that doesn't steal valuable space from bedrooms.

◄ Pay attention to detail. Carefully selected accessories, added with care and flair, can add tremendously to the value of your home. Light switches, door handles, light fittings, taps, cornices, skirting boards and the like, are all important in this respect.

◄ Out with the old. Consider replacing worn-out carpets with more modern floorcoverings, such as coir carpets, new tiles or gleaming wood.

◄ Spacious and inviting. Knock out unnecessary dividing walls. A spacious open-plan kitchen and dining room will hold more appeal than two separate rooms divided by unnecessary walls and doors.

◄ Safety and security. Burglar-proofed windows, an alarm and sensor lights offer peace of mind and add to the overall value of the house.

◄ Special features. Extras such as a fireplace, underfloor heating, covered parking, a built-in braai, a jacuzzi, sauna, electric garage doors and a garden irrigation system all add welcome value to a house.

◄ Repair and replace. Consider fitting new windows and replacing rusted or warped frames with new wood or aluminium frames if a lot of damage has been done by the weather. Make sure the new frames blend well with the style of the house.

◄ Add a room. If you live in an area where space is at a premium or where there is a significant price difference between three- and four-bedroom homes, consider converting the roof space into a loft area. Find out if you need planning permission and building regulations approval.

◄ First impressions count. Well-maintained woodwork and a freshly painted exterior with no broken gutters and loose roof tiles will ensure that your house creates a good first impression.

◄ A tidy garden. A well-designed and well-maintained garden will add to the overall appearance and appeal of the property.

◄ Maximise natural light. Where possible, enlarge small windows that let in very little natural light. If you can't enlarge a small window, consider installing skylights. Bright and sunny rooms appear more spacious and are open and inviting.

◄ Choose colours carefully. When choosing paint colours for walls, keep in mind that dark colours will make a room appear smaller. You will do well to opt for light and neutral tones.

◄ Simplest basics. Don't despair if your budget does not allow for elaborate improvement projects. One of the best ways to add value to your home is also one of the cheapest. A tidy house, a well-kept garden and a fresh coat of paint will add to the appeal of any house, and make it easier for buyers to see what a property has to offer.

Making simple improvements won't necessarily add thousands to the selling price of a house, but it can help a sale to go through, and make it more likely that the buyer pays very close to the asking price. There is one golden rule you should follow when making any improvements: whatever you do, do it well. No one wants to pay for shoddy workmanship, and quality will almost always hold its value in the long term. Go for the best you can afford!

steer clear

The following could detract from the value of a house, and should be avoided or improved upon:

◄ unfinished or botched DIY jobs
◄ a darkly coloured bathroom suite
◄ too many extensions
◄ an unkempt garden
◄ stained carpets and walls
◄ outlandish decorations

You've found the perfect house to make your home. It needs a little work, but there are just enough bedrooms and the kitchen has real potential ... Before you buy a house, make sure that you know what it entails, from your agent's duties to financing the renovations.

Choosing and buying a house

Location

'Location, location, location' is more than just a clichéd catch phrase. The area in which your property (or the property you are interested in) is situated, has a substantial influence on its current value, as well as its potential to increase in value. You should take it upon yourself to investigate an area in which you are interested. Don't just take an agent or seller's word for it when they profess an area to be the next posh neighbourhood, waiting to be discovered.

Take a drive around the area during different times of the day. Look at key issues such as safety, traffic, the proximity of shopping centres, hospitals and schools. What is public transport like in the area?

Look at the neighbourhood and the people who live there. What type of neighbourhood is it? Do the people seem friendly, or noisy, or do they seem to be concerned that an unfamiliar vehicle is driving up and down their streets?

Find out about any planned developments in the area. Make sure that they won't detract from the value of the property.

The house itself

Before you start negotiating with the seller or the agent, make sure that the rooms offer quality space. The curved wall between the lounge and the kitchen might look quite arty now, but will the room be able to accommodate all your furniture, and will you be able to utilise the wall effectively?

Make sure that the rooms are in proportion. There's little use in having a kitchen the size of a one-man tent and a bathroom the size of a school hall. Make sure that the rooms all lead off a hallway and that you don't need to walk through one room to access another.

Check that the garden is a manageable size, that it offers privacy, and is secure. And, of course, look at the aspect of the house, i.e. which direction it faces, and how much sunlight it receives.

The estate agent

If you are serious about a house, you will need to make use of an estate agent who will negotiate the sale. Even after you have signed an offer to purchase, and the seller has accepted it, the estate agent will continue to play a role.

Real estate agents should be able to answer any of your questions related to the house and the area. If they can't answer your questions, at the very least they should be in a position to find the answers on your behalf.

Although a house cannot be sold with a guarantee, the agent does have the responsibility of showing the house as transparently as possible.

Buyers should be warned about the pitfalls in terms of latent and patent defects. A patent defect is clearly visible to any reasonable person inspecting the property, and the seller is not liable for these. A latent defect is one that is not visible or easily noticeable upon inspection, for example, a leaking roof, damp, or structural defects in the foundations. The seller is liable for latent defects that existed when the contract was signed, even if he was unaware of them.

If a latent defect is found, the buyer is legally entitled to institute a claim against the seller. These claims are always against the seller, and not the agent.

It is essential and in both parties' interests that the contract includes a 'voetstoots' clause that excludes the seller's liability for defects. However, this clause does not exclude the seller's liability if he/she was aware of the defect and purposely withheld the information in order to defraud the buyer.

Check list

Make a list of everything that needs to be connected, such as water and lights. If you have a satellite dish, don't forget to make arrangements for it to be disconnected and reinstalled at your new property.

Avoid moving-in and moving-out clashes, and ask about occupation dates, as well as the keys. Make sure that you know which items are included with the house. Have these detailed and put in writing on the offer to purchase. Ask about items, such as water filters, plants and containers in the garden or on the patio, garden tools and the garden shed, as well as the pool and its cleaning equipment. Ask if the swimming pool pump is working

ask these questions

When you're viewing a house, ask lots of questions about it, and examine everything closely. Eager buyers often make the mistake of signing for a house, without having done very much investigation. You're even entitled to ask professionals to assess the condition of certain aspects of the house, should you wish to do so.

As a prospective buyer you need to ask pertinent questions about any aspect or issue that concerns you, or about which you are concerned. The questions you should ask include the following:

◄ Where are the nearest highways?

◄ Are there any development plans for the neighbourhood, of which we need to be aware?

◄ Are there any servitudes through or on the property that we should know about?

◄ If it is a semi-detached house, ask whether there is a fire wall between the adjoining properties (not only as a security measure, but also to protect your property against fire damage from the neighbouring property).

◄ Have the electrical and pest certificates been arranged?

◄ Which are fixtures and which are not fixtures of the house?

◄ Does the house have damp?

◄ How old is the house?

◄ What is the security like? Is there a neighbourhood watch?

◄ What are the municipal rates?

◄ What are the levies (in the case of a sectional title home)?

◄ Are there any other property defects that the seller knows about?

◄ Has the seller recently repaired any defects and are there any guarantees on any of these repairs?

◄ Are the original building plans still available?

and, if applicable, make sure that it is. Ask whether the Kreepy Krawly or Barracuda is included.

Also check with the local authority to ascertain whether the house you're interested in buying corresponds with the title deeds or house plans that they have on file. If a previous owner made some alterations without getting the plans approved, you will be liable for costs if a structure has to be removed or has been built outside the parameters of your property.

Legal issues and fees

The buyer needs to know for which legal fees he or she is liable, on purchasing the property. The buyer also needs to be aware that the seller has the right to appoint the conveyancing attorneys handling the transfer of the property.

According to South African Property Law, nothing has legal substance if it's not in writing. Therefore, what is agreed upon, must be listed, put in writing and signed by all parties concerned. Verbal agreements simply don't stand up in court.

As the buyer making an offer to purchase, you should ensure that, if the deal is 'subject to' certain conditions, there is a cut-off point by which these need to be fulfilled; after this date your offer to purchase should be reviewed.

Also, all occupational rental details must be finalised before the offer to purchase is signed. The agent should not cross this out, but should examine all the possible scenarios and record the details agreed upon.

Sectional title deals

It is important for the buyer to understand that, by buying a sectional title home, he or she is actually investing in two things: his/her own unit, and a share in the common property. The buyer once again needs to ask a whole series of questions with regard to the common property, such as what exactly it includes.

With regard to the upkeep of the common property, a special levy may be instituted every three or four years, for example for painting, security fencing, etc.

The buyer needs to ask for details on how often the special levy is instituted and what flexibility is provided for in terms of the payment of these levies.

If you're interested in buying a sectional title home, make sure that the scheme is in good financial health. Some schemes have arrears in levy collection, and the new buyers often find themselves paying increased levies soon after moving in. Ask about the Body Corporate, and to whom the levies should be paid. Find out about the Body Corporate insurance coverage. Be sure to check which party pays for the development's security, and whether you will be billed extra.

The agent must supply you with a copy of the Special Rules of the Body Corporate, and must also point out which garage(s) apply to the home, as well as any free parking areas.

Be wire wise

Purchasing 'off plan', buyers are often given the opportunity to choose their own carpets, tiles, cabinets and counter tops. But they're seldom, if ever, consulted about anything electrical or electronic in nature – even in this age of home computers, satellite TV, and fridges that can connect to the Internet.

Today, one of the best investments you will ever make, is to have your home properly 'wired' for modern communications, entertainment and security systems – while it's still under construction. Doing this should eliminate the need for duplicate equipment, complex hook-ups and trailing extensions, not to mention the disruption and inconvenience of having additional wiring installed at a later stage.

It may be worth asking your developer or builder if you could scale down on the more cosmetic 'fitting and finishing' options, in favour of any or all of the following:

◀ additional sockets for computers, your home theatre system and kitchen appliances
◀ a 'clean' power supply for your home computer/s
◀ allowance for extra telephone jacks
◀ additional TV aerial connections in specified rooms
◀ some type of accommodation for your satellite dish
◀ multiple-outlet satellite TV connection
◀ additional, wired-in speakers for a music system
◀ wiring for your security system's movement sensors, panic buttons, and closed-circuit door or gate cameras.

Creating your dream home

Financing improvements

Revamping your kitchen or building an extension might be all that is needed to transform your house into a dream home. Plan your finances carefully, ensure that you pay as little interest as possible, and don't compromise your financial health. There are several financing options you could consider.

◀ **Overdraft**

Used to finance relatively small amounts, you need a cheque account to qualify. The amount you're granted will depend on your income and credit history. You can apply for a temporary overdraft of a few months, or a permanent overdraft. Permanent overdraft is usually granted for a period of one year, and then renewed. Interest will be charged.

◀ **Personal loan**

Generally, you need a fixed monthly income, sound cash flow, and a good credit record. You may also need security (such as a policy with a surrender or cash value, or unit trusts). It is repayable over one to five years and you may need to take out life assurance to cover the loan in the event of your death, or you becoming critically ill, etc. Find out as much as possible regarding the terms of the loan, such as the period over which it has to be repaid, fixed interest rates, and so on.

◀ **Building loan**

The number of payments is decided beforehand, and the bank makes progress payments as each stage is completed. The bank ensures that properly registered builders are used, and monitors the project to make sure it's finished within a reasonable time.

◀ **Home loans**

Modern home loans are flexible and can be tailored to pay for your renovations, usually at a lower interest rate than on other types of loans.

If you're applying for a home loan, your monthly repayment should not be more than 30% of your single or joint gross monthly income. You will have to pass a credit record check, and the interest rate will be assessed according to your needs and means. Interest is calculated on the outstanding daily balance and debited monthly.

◀ Register a higher bond than you think you'll need and make use of the surplus amount for renovating. This does not mean you pay more at first, as you will pay interest only on the borrowed amount. When it is time to renovate, you will have the finance available.

◀ Apply for a re-advance on your home loan. This will extend the loan period without the costs of legal fees or registering a new bond. The amount you can access depends on how much you've already paid off – you can borrow up to the original loan amount.

◀ Apply for an additional home loan. This is the most expensive option because it involves valuing the property to assess whether the extension is worthwhile. There will be bond registration costs and the bank will do an affordability test to check that you can make the payments.

Regardless of which loan you choose, do your budgeting very carefully. Don't get carried away and take on too much debt. Ask as many questions as you need to make an informed decision. Pay the loan off as soon as possible, and always keep your bank informed of any changes to the original plan.

Renovate, improve, replace

Renovating your home by expanding it or adding your personal touch can be more than just a distant dream. With careful planning, both in terms of lifestyle and financial considerations, you can live in the house you've always wanted. In addition, making the right improvements will increase the value of your investment.

However, you need to know where to draw the line between making improvements that add value and quality of life, and spending a fortune just to make the house liveable. This is particularly important and relevant if you're in the market for, or have already invested in an older home.

Valuable original features

Fortunately, not all older homes are the worse for wear. Many have been well-maintained over the years, and prove to be real finds – often because of their highly sought-after and very valuable original features. If you've bought an older home or are interested in buying one, be on the lookout for original features. These could be anything from wooden floors and intricate banisters to fireplaces and exceptional wooden doors. For example, if the house has a chimney stack but no apparent fireplace, chances are that it's been plastered over by one of the previous owners. Tap the wall and listen for hollow sounds that could indicate the position of the fireplace.

In Victorian homes, lower ceilings could be suspended ceilings that are masking the original cornicing. Compare the relative position of the windows to the ceiling. A hidden cellar can be detected by looking at the outside walls – if there are vents where there shouldn't be, chances are you've found the cellar. Alternatively, look for doorways that might have been blocked off, which could originally have led to the cellar.

In older homes it's also important to establish what can be restored, and what should rather be replaced.

Be realistic

As mentioned before, it is important to know when to draw the line when it comes to renovating, redecorating and improving a home. Don't overcapitalise (i.e. when the cost of the renovation is more than the value it will add to the property). For example, if you add a top-of-the-range kitchen worth R50 000 to a house worth R200 000, it is unlikely that you'd recoup that expense when selling the house, and thus you've overcapitalised.

Think carefully about the effects that renovations and improvements will have on the resale value of your house. A sauna, for instance, might suit your lifestyle and be within your budget, but very few potential buyers will appreciate this addition or be willing to pay either the expense of its maintenance or the cost of its removal.

Once you've considered and prioritised the renovations and improvements that will not only enhance your lifestyle but also add to the value of your investment, make sure that your funds will cover all of these modifications.

If you're still paying off your bond, examine your budget carefully and ensure that you are able to cover costs before you undertake any renovations. After all, you wouldn't want to start renovating your kitchen only to find that you cannot complete it. At the same time, the last thing you want to do is get yourself too deeply into debt.

Once your finances are in order, shop around for the best suppliers and find the most cost-effective materials.

Pitfalls to consider

Some common pitfalls to avoid when renovating include:

‹ **Buying the wrong property**

Property adjoining or within shabby neighbourhoods, cannot be saved by expensive renovations.

‹ **Misunderstanding the local property market**

Consider talking to any estate agent, ask who the potential buyers in your area are, what it is that they look for. Then decide how to renovate.

‹ **Inadequate cost and time management**

Careful planning is essential if you wish to remain in control of time spent on the job, and expenditures.

‹ **A botched DIY job**

Before you decide to do something yourself, make sure you know exactly what you're doing. A botched DIY job can seriously devalue the appeal of your home.

Getting started

Once you've established that you have adequate funding for a major renovation or a home improvement job, you will need to start enquiring about builders or other artisans who will be able to assist you to complete the task in such a way that it looks professional and adds real value to your home.

Don't ever simply accept the lowest quote or ask only for two quotes and then accept whichever one seems more reasonable. Quotes are usually free, so get as many as you can and make thorough comparisons. Ideally, you should select a builder who is registered with a professional body such as the Master Builder's Association (MBA), the Building Industries Association (BIA), the Industrial Council for the Building Industry (ICBI) or the National Association of Home Builders (NAHB). Phone one of these bodies for a professional recommendation – their members are skilled, financially stable and have an ethical approach to their work. Builders are not obliged to belong to any of these organisations, but if they do, it does give you some protection, and them some credibility.

Do not underestimate the value of word-of-mouth references and recommendations from friends or acquaintances who have had restoration work done. Ideally you should also choose a builder with a few years' experience and who can show you an updated portfolio of his work. The only way to judge the quality of workmanship effectively is through an on-site inspection. Ask the builder for names of recent clients and arrange to take a look at these projects.

Builder's questionnaire

If you've found a builder that you are seriously considering using, do a background check (especially if he was not recommended to you, i.e. you found him in the Yellow Pages), and then ask him the following questions:

◄ How long has he been a building contractor?
◄ Does he work full time or part time?
◄ Is he registered with any of the bodies mentioned above?
◄ How many projects similar to yours has he completed?
◄ Ask for reference names and numbers of his last five clients.
◄ Does he have insurance?

◄ Who will be doing the actual work?
◄ Does his quote seem reasonable?
◄ Can he draw up plans and get them passed?
◄ What are his regular work hours?
◄ Will he provide his own contract?

Once you've found and decided upon using a specific builder, do keep the following in mind. It cannot be stressed enough that the lowest quotation is not necessarily always the best one. If a builder's quote is more than 20 percent less than the majority of the other quotes you received, you definitely have to question why. Also be wary of a builder who will accept only cash or asks for a lot of cash upfront. You should not be paying for services that are yet to be rendered. Consider giving him a miss if there is no letterhead or address on his quote, or a VAT registration number. Be equally suspicious of any builder who insists that you do not need planning permission from your local authority and avoid a builder who is afraid of having his work inspected.

keep in mind

◄ Modernising an existing kitchen and adding a new bathroom are the most value-adding changes you can make to your home. Keep this in mind when you have to decide between modernising the kitchen and adding another bedroom.

◄ Ensure that no alterations (especially strucutural) negatively affect the structural integrity of the house. Make sure that you (and your builder) understand the impact of the changes or the extension, before you start any work.

◄ If possible, consult a structural engineer about the effects that alterations will have on the structure of your house. He'll be able to work out, for example, if rainwater drainage will be able to follow its natural course after the alteration, or whether the slope of a new roof will cause the courtyard to be very windy.

◄ During the construction phase, extra work (that is not covered in the original quote) might need to be done. Obtain quotes before any work is carried out.

Doing a home makeover can be a nerve-wracking experience. The fear of making costly mistakes often deters people from taking on exciting projects that just seem too complicated. With proper planning, however, no makeover experience should be distressing and no project impossible.

planning

Proper planning is essential for any makeover and decorating project to be a success. It will allow you to experiment without paying a fortune, and will lower any risks involved. When planning is overlooked or not done properly, you can almost be sure of a disastrous result. This chapter shows you how and where the process of proper planning starts. You will learn how to assess your needs and wants, which in turn will enable you to know how and which changes need to be made to your home. You will learn how to create balance and add character to a room, and discover your personal preferences by creating mood boards and experimenting with various textures, colours and styles.

Make a plan

Setting out and starting off with a good plan will keep you on track and ensure that you get the job done – on time and within the budget. It will highlight possible pitfalls, and enable you to divide major projects into manageable steps.

How to plan

1. Establish your needs and wants

How much time do you spend at home? Do you have a family? Do you entertain? Do you spend weekends at home, or do you travel often? Think about the functions you want your house to fulfil. Consider how your life might change in the near future: gran might need a room soon, or the students might be thinking of moving out. Draw up a list of what you need, and allocate rooms accordingly. This will give you a clear picture of where you want to be, and make getting it right that much easier.

2. Make an assessment

After drawing up your list, take a slow walk through your house. Think about how you can change it to meet your needs and wants. Do you have carpeting that you seldom have the time to clean? Do you need a second bathroom? Does the family room need doors leading out onto the garden, or does it need a new couch? Is security what it should be? List everything that can be altered or improved to suit your needs. Perhaps you only need to make minor cosmetic changes, or perhaps your home needs major remodelling that involves extensive building. Take note of ALL the things that need attention – nicks in the wall, sagging upholstery, rusty windows, broken tiles, ceilings in need of paint, etc.

3. List projects according to your budget

Visit various building suppliers to see what is available and compare prices. Get quotes from reputable builders or handymen (for the things you can't do yourself) and write it all down in a project book to refer back to. Work out approximately how much everything will cost and match that to your budget.

Stagger the projects according to your budget, listing crucial ones first and purely decorative ones last. Decide what will be the best immediate change and, if possible, slot that in near the top. Group together projects that can be done simultaneously, whether they are similar or simply in the same room.

It is best to start with major building work (such as repairing, replacing or adding to your structure), as this will involve the most costly and unsettling changes. Only once the major building work has been done, can the decorating begin. As tempted as you may be, do not start making superficial changes before all the major ones have been completed – doing so just might break the bank.

4. Draw up a plan

List the projects according to priority; then draw up a plan of what you want to do, what you will need and when you want to start. Note these days in your diary and try not to schedule anything else during this time. Take the weather into account and, if possible, try not to plan any major building projects during the rainy season of your particular region.

Before starting any project, make sure you have absolutely all the right tools and materials needed for the job. Study the project instructions carefully and make sure you know exactly what to do and how to do it. If possible, enlist the help of a friend or handyman to speed up the process.

5. Start

Stick to your schedule as best you can, and consult a professional if you're faced with a problem you cannot solve.

Room by room

Tackle projects room by room. You'll be able to see progress and results more clearly, and to continue as the budget allows. Trying to redo the entire house in one go will only result in chaos – especially if you run out of funds halfway through.

To the drawing board

Working with small-scale drawings is a good starting point – whether you want to make structural changes to an existing room, are building a new room, or are simply redecorating. It is an easy way of creating interesting settings that you might not have thought of otherwise, and will help you determine which pieces of furniture will be the most practical choice in terms of size and dimension. The best way to go about it is to work in millimetres – a scale of 1:50 is a comfortable size that will fit well onto an A4-sheet of paper.

Measuring your room

Measure the length and width of your room in millimetres, and make a rough drawing of the room accordingly. Measure and note the size and position of the windows, doors, and other existing features (such as a fireplace, serving hatch and built-in shelving). Measure the distance between each feature, as well as the distance between each feature and the nearest corner of the room. Divide each measurement by 50, converting it to a smaller scale. Now make an accurate drawing of your room according to these measurements, carefully placing the fixed features.

Measure each piece of furniture you want to use in the room. Work in millimetres and reduce the measurements as before. Make basic drawings according to the reduced measurements (on scrap paper or coloured card) and cut them out neatly. Position them on the scale drawing to work out what will fit where, or to find a whole new lay-out for the room.

Use the same method to draw an entire house or flat, and have fun experimenting with the various ways in which you can arrange your furniture.

Size versus space

Don't assume that a small room needs small furniture – this often only creates a busy and cluttered look. Fewer, and bigger items will allow more room for movement, while simultaneously creating the illusion of more space.

basic standard measurements (in millimetres)

lounge suite

SINGLE-SEATER	900 x 1 000
TWO-SEATER	900 x 1 700
THREE-SEATER	900 x 2 500

beds

SINGLE	910 x 1 880
THREE-QUARTER	1 070 x 1 880
DOUBLE	1 370 x 1 880
QUEEN SIZE	1 520 x 1 880
KING SIZE	1 830 x 1 880
EXTRA-LONG	length = 2 000

kitchen storage and appliances

BUILT-IN CUPBOARDS: Door sizes vary according to the measurements of the room and the number of cupboards.

The general depth of floor-standing cupboards is 600 mm, and 300 mm for wall-mounted cupboards.

FRIDGE	600 x 650
FREEZER	600 x 650
HOB	600 x 600; 650 x 650; 750 x 650
DISHWASHER	600 x 600
FRONT-LOADER WASHING MACHINES AND TUMBLE DRYERS	
	600 x 600

bathroom suite

BATH	1 700 x 750
DOUBLE BASIN	1 200 x 600
SINGLE BASIN	600 x 400
SHOWER	900 x 900
TOILET	750 x 575

Focal points

A focal point is that which initially catches your eye and draws your attention as you enter a room. It can be anything from a beautiful window, or a wall painted in a striking colour, to a piece of furniture, or an antique mirror.

Focal points are generally used to create the mood and feel of a room, and can therefore dictate the choice of furniture and accessories that go with it.

They are also often existing features, for example, an old fireplace or a striking bay window. Older houses usually have one or more such features, making it easy work when deciding what to accentuate. Modern houses, on the other hand, quite often don't have these classic features that draw the eye and influence the way the room is perceived, so you will have to choose and create your own.

Focal points need to vary in size and shape, and have different visual impacts – too many similar objects calling for attention will only confuse the eye and you won't know where to look. Rather choose a larger item or surface to set the scene, then carry it through with a few well-chosen pieces of furniture and accessories to create a balance.

Walk around your room and note which elements are worthy of accentuating, and whether they will add the right feel to the overall effect that you wish to create. Striking accessories, or a few interesting objects placed together, also work well as focal points that can be planned into the basic room lay-out.

By using focal points correctly, and following the flow of the room, you can lead someone through it by providing interesting touches along the way. In small spaces a single focal point is adequate; too many will only clutter the space.

If your room has no fixed features, decide whether you want to accentuate a wall or use a striking piece of furniture to do the trick. Alternatively, use both one wall and a piece of furniture as focal points that complement each other. An antique bed or cupboard, for example, will instantly provide a romantic feel in the bedroom, and could further be complemented with a pastel-pink focal wall, and a bedside mirror with antique crystal detail.

Focal points can be used to accentuate a specific theme or style in a room. For example, arrange a few striking Eastern-inspired accessories in the bedroom and balance them with a brightly painted focal wall. Or, build a faux fireplace to add an edge to the understated, modern feel of a stylish lounge.

Creating focal points

You can create a focal point either by adding something to or by taking something away from a feature. Curtains, for example, will draw attention away from a bay window, while an inviting window seat will only add to its appeal. A beautifully detailed fireplace will be lost underneath excessive clutter and should be cleared of any unnecessary objects. You can display a few striking vases on a mantelpiece and hang a large mirror above it to draw attention. Or group pictures, mirrors and interesting artefacts together in an attractive manner on the wall above the mantelpiece. Group elements neatly if you prefer a formal look, or loosely if you like a more relaxed, lived-in feel.

Beautifully shaped furniture and accessories can also be used as focal points. Use a large free-standing cupboard, a couch, or a very striking single chair to draw attention, and place the piece where it can easily be seen. Consider painting the backing wall in a complementary colour, or hang a mirror, a picture or a painting above it to accentuate the colour or the shape of the furniture. Clear unnecessary clutter, cushions and ornaments, or arrange them artfully to add to the charm of the piece.

Style tip

Focal points are used to communicate the style and feel of a room. Clear anything that is not complementary or that simply clashes with everything else. You will see other elements, which you might not have noticed before, come into their own.

Opposite This striking mirror arrangement is a simple and effective focal point that has the added advantage of reflecting light into the room. The reflection of the room also creates the illusion of more space.

Mood boards

What is a mood board?

Also known as a story board, the mood board is the interior decorator's tool of choice and is used to compile the story of a room or home. Simply put, it is a summary or suggested summary of all the fabric samples, paint colours, floorcoverings and carpeting that work well together, and that could be implemented should you like the result.

Creating a mood board of your own will help you make informed decisions, and avoid costly mistakes. It will also teach you more about your own style and colour preferences. Most importantly, a mood board will enable you to decorate with confidence, because it will give you a very good idea of what the end result is going to look like.

Style tip

Although it was once highly fashionable to decorate every room in a house in a different style and colour, the current trend is more towards creating unity within the home by using only one basic style and palette. Rooms are decorated in different ways, and in various hues of the same palette, while still combining with and complementing the main style of the house.

Make a mood board for your home and choose the most suitable style and colour scheme. Follow with smaller, complementary mood boards for each of the individual rooms.

create your own mood board

You will need:

✓ a piece of cardboard
✓ décor magazines
✓ scissors
✓ paint strips
✓ fabric and carpeting samples
✓ glue

1. Slowly page through the magazines and cut out all the images and colours that catch your eye. Look carefully at everything – carpets, blinds, curtains, bedding, beds and more, and cut out whatever takes your fancy.
2. Once you have worked your way through quite a few magazines and you have a number of cut-outs, spread them out in front of you. You should be able to see a general trend towards certain colours and feels being repeated. These should give you a good indication of the styles and colours that you truly like. Use this as your starting block.

3. The next step is to pop into your local hardware store, fabric showroom and carpet specialist for paint strips, fabric swatches and carpeting samples that will match or complement your existing story.
4. Play around with all the cut-outs and samples until you find just the right colours and combinations. Position your choice of carpeting at the bottom of the piece of cardboard, and place the furniture around the middle section. Position the curtains, blinds and lighting near the top. Keep it proportionate to the area it will cover, or cut or fold down to size if necessary.
5. Glue all the cut-outs and samples into place. Write down the codes, prices and suppliers' details on a seperate piece of paper. Attach this to the back of your mood board for easy access.

You should now have a very good idea of how well everything works together. If you are still not happy with the result, change it with new samples and cut-outs until you are completely satisfied. Leave no carpet sample unturned!

When you hold all the boards together, the general feel and colours should blend and complement each other well. Any harsh variations should be toned down or blended in carefully to ensure continuity throughout.

Start with what you like

If you know what it is that you like and what you dislike, but have no idea where to start or which colours and furnishings to choose, don't despair. Take a sample of something that you really like, for example, a piece of upholstery, an interesting rug, or a favourite painting, and create a mood board around it. Experiment by adding various colours and textures until you find just the right combination to use.

Using your mood board

Once you are happy with your mood board, go back to the various stockists and ask for larger sample materials. Make a summary of what you are planning: place the carpeting on the floor, and drape the fabric over your furniture or peg it up in front of the window. Paint a small section of the wall or paint a sheet of paper in the sample colour and stick this to the wall.

Stand back, take a good look, and imagine the overall effect it will have. Doing this will allow you to see your mood board in context, and will enable you to see if what works well on paper, will work in reality as well. Leave it there for a day or two; let it grow on you, or see whether you tire of it quickly. Also take note of the effect of morning versus afternoon light.

The most important part of any makeover is the basics. The type and colour of paint you use, the floorcovering, and the finishing touches you add, all form part of its cosmetic foundation. A good foundation will deliver positive results, and a makeover with real long-term value.

the basics

Your home is probably the biggest single investment you will ever make. It is also the one place where you're allowed to do as you please. It's where you spend most of your time with family and friends, and a place where you feel safe and secure.

'Home' could be a two-bedroomed flat in the centre of town, a three-bedroomed house in the leafy lanes of a suburb, a wooden cottage in the country, or a double-storey mansion overlooking the ocean. Whatever the size or the location of the space that you have, you will need to invest in it to make it your perfect home. The best investment you will ever make, is an investment in the basics, the cosmetic foundations of your home.

Whether you're improving the look of your home, or simply refreshing an outdated style, don't rush into anything. Before you get your hands dirty, take time to think about the basic lay-out of your home, how the rooms fit together, which original features you would like to keep, and where services such as electrical points and drains are or should be.

Wall wonders

Pattern and texture are the two elements to consider when choosing wallcoverings. They are available in virtually any colour and pattern imagineable.

Wallcoverings range from the simplest colours with minimal texture to intricate murals with multiple colours. Wallcoverings can be made of paper, cork, wood, metal, vinyl and a variety of other synthetic textiles.

Choosing a wall finish

Wallpaper is more appropriate for use in low traffic areas that do not need regular maintenance. It is more delicate than vinyl, but is nevertheless quite durable, and adds interest to any room. Modern wallpaper designs can be quite expensive, however, and applying wallpaper is not always simple and easy. Bear this in mind when making your final decision.

You should always consider durability when choosing a wall finish. Different wall finishes will work better in certain areas, for example, wallpaper will better suit a study than a kitchen or a bathroom. Decide for which purpose you would like to use a room, before you settle on a wallcovering.

Synthetic textile wallcoverings can be extremely durable and may be made from one, or a combination of materials.

Keep the following in mind when you choose a wallcovering:

◄ Is it washable and can you scrub it if it gets dirty?
◄ Will it wear off quickly if exposed to high traffic?
◄ Will it tear easily, for example if children play in the room?
◄ Is it stain-resistant, and will it crack easily?

If you use a wallcovering in a room like a bathroom or kitchen, make sure that it can withstand extreme temperatures and humid conditions. Also check that it is resistant to mildew and damp.

In bathrooms, especially, walls must be able to withstand high condensation. This is no place for unsealed plaster or unfinished wood, as these will eventually be damaged by the extreme humidity. Keep in mind that bathroom walls frequently need to be wiped down and cleaned. Make sure that the wall-covering you choose will be able to withstand these conditions.

Paint basics

Paint provides an effective, simple and quick finish for all surfaces. To ensure good results, you need to know which paint to use where, and how to prepare the surface properly. To ensure long-lasting results, always prepare a surface thoroughly, and invest in good quality paint.

Painting is a labour-intensive and costly exercise, so you cannot afford to make mistakes. Use the right materials and don't be tempted to be too fashionable with your choice of colours. Hot pink may look great on the pages of a glossy magazine, but will you be able to live with it for the next five years? This is the time for good planning and sensible decision making.

To DIY or not to DIY

Before painting, consult a knowledgeable, specialist supplier, especially when selecting primers and other materials. If you are in doubt, weigh up the risks against the cost of using a professional painter.

Paint: what to use and where to use it

Repainting your house is a substantial investment. Top-quality paints will double the life expectancy of the paint job, reducing maintenance costs and ultimately saving thousands of rands.

◄ Double Velvet is an interior paint with a sheen finish. It is a washable and stain-resistant; low-odour, quick-drying and non-yellowing paint. Use it on new cement plaster walls, fibreboard, ceiling board, plaster, metal and wood.
◄ Cashmere is an interior paint with an ultra-matt finish. It is washable and stain resistant.
◄ Velvaglo is an interior and exterior, non-drip, hard-wearing enamel. It is oil-based and has a protective semi-gloss finish. Ideal for use on primed woodwork, plaster or metal.
◄ Velvaglo Gloss is an oil-based, high-gloss protective finish. It is suitable for both interior and exterior use on primed woodwork, plaster or metal.
◄ Wall 'n All is an exterior wall coating that is washable, durable, and dirt resistant.
◄ Polvin Super Acrylic PVA is an interior acrylic emulsion. Use it on plaster, concrete, porous brickwork and building boards.

◄ Eggshell, gloss and stainwood are hard-wearing, easy to clean and ideal for woodwork. These finishes work well in rooms with high humidity and condensation. Gloss takes ages to dry, so keep the area dust-free. It's not ideal for walls.

◄ Laquer is a more glamorous alternative to gloss and has a shinier finish. Although it can be used on walls, it is mostly used on wood.

◄ Limewash gives a velvety finish that allows walls to breathe.

◄ Kitchen and bathroom paints often include a fungicide to discourage fungal growth in humid places. Use acrylic eggshell paints with a tough, washable finish that is resistant to staining from household cleaners.

◄ Super Universal Enamel is oil-based, has a high-gloss finish, and can be used on interior and exterior surfaces.

◄ One-coat paints are designed to be applied slightly thicker than regular paint, offering adequate coverage in a single application. If you're painting over dark colours, however, it's likely that you'll still need to apply two coats.

◄ Satin-finish paints have a subtle sheen finish. Use eggshell on walls, as an alternative to standard matt emulsions; on woodwork, use a stainwood product for a more understated finish.

◄ Water-based paints are low-odour, easy to clean off brushes, rollers and clothing, and dry fast.

◄ Primers and sealants are available for use on surfaces such as melamine or metal.

◄ Exterior masonry paint has additives that make it weather-proof; it is used to cover brick or concrete.

Always use quality paint

Good quality paint might seem a little expensive at first, but in the long run, it will cost you much less than buying a cheap paint of inferior quality.

For example, a quality paint will provide good coverage, which means you will use less paint than you would should you buy the cheaper paint that offers inferior coverage because of its poor quality. Using poor quality paint usually also means you have to apply numerous coats where one or two applications should have been enough.

Estimate the quantity

Measure the length of each wall, add together, then multiply this figure by the height of the room to give the area in square metres. Then check the side of your paint tin for the recommended coverage (square metres) per litre.

The right tools for the job

Rollers give walls a professional finish. Use short-haired rollers for smooth walls and a longer pile for rough areas. Buy a roller with a screw thread in the handle so you can add an extension pole.

Pads in foam or mohair are great for painting large areas with oil-based paints, and give a smooth finish to flat areas. They don't splatter the paint like a roller, but they're also not as quick.

Brushes are essential for working around the edges of a wall or ceiling, and for narrow window frames and door mouldings. Tapered bristles give a more even spread of paint than same-length bristles. For water-based, quick-drying paint, choose synthetic bristles. A small bristle brush with an angled top is perfect for narrow beading.

What to wear

When attempting any paint job, a long-sleeved overall and a pair of old tackies will offer you the best protection. Alternatively, wear an old sweater and old jeans. Use to these every time you paint. Don't think you can do a quick job wearing your favourite pants, top or shoes. No matter how carefully you work, you will get paint on either one, or all of these items. Invest in a pair of gloves, especially if you have a sensitive skin or are prone to allergies. When painting flooring, invest in kneeguards to protect your knees; protect your hair by wearing a cap or a bandana.

How to remove paint

Water-based paint is best removed (immediately) with soap and water. For oil-based paint spills, use turpentine.

tip
Wear an apron with a pocket over your overall and keep a cloth in the pocket for unexpected paint spills!

Choosing the right colour

When selecting colours, always keep the age and character of your home in mind. The colour range available is virtually unlimited, but before you rush out and ask your local paint stockist to mix you 100 litres of the season's hottest shade, buy only a very small quantity and paint a test patch on your wall. In fact, buy a few different colours and test them all.

Paint a square metre or so of each of the colours on the desired surface, and live with them for a few days before making a final decision.

Build up a collection of sample cards when choosing your paint colour. A colour wheel will be an invaluable tool that will help you to select co-ordinating and contrasting colours, and much much more.

Colours that heat and cool

The aspect of a room and the size and position of its windows will affect how light or dark the room is, and whether it feels warm and golden, or cold and grey. This will have an effect on any colours you wish to paint the room.

Cool room

A cool room is one that receives little direct sunlight and always appears cold. You get a similar effect when the windows are small, and the room doesn't receive enough natural light. If the room is gloomy for most of the day, and there are deep shadows in corners and under furniture, you can be certain it is a cold room.

What to do: Introduce warmer colours such as yellow, orange, red and brown to give it a warming effect. Don't paint this room stark white or ice blue as these colours will accentuate its coolness.

Warm room

These rooms usually have large windows, receive plenty of light and appear particularly warm and golden in the morning or evening. If the room is dazzlingly bright with a golden hue, you can be certain it is a warm room.

What to do: Balance the room with cool colours such as blue, aqua, turquoise and green.

Neutral room

These rooms receive adequate natural light that is fairly constant throughout the day. They often have windows on opposite or adjacent walls. If the room is flooded with light and the light intensity remains the same throughout the day, you can be certain it is a neutral room.

What to do: These rooms can take almost any kind of colour scheme, but take care that the effect is not too flat and bland.

Colour schemes

No matter what your colour preferences, once you understand the basic rules of colour, choosing the right colours for a room or home becomes easy.

Neutrals

This scheme is based on soft, earthy neutrals such as white, beige, wood tones and grey. It works with classic and modern designs and is always a stylish choice.

Monochromatic

This colour scheme, based around one colour used in different shades and tints, brings movement to the space in a room.

Primary colours

Only use primary colours (red, blue or yellow) on one wall in a room to make a statement. Balance it with a softer shade such as white. When using one of the three primary colours, tone it down with a softer hue that acts as background to these vibrant accents.

Complementary

Choose colours from the opposite sides of the colour wheel, such as blue and orange, for a balanced colour scheme.

Opposite Warm and vibrant colours have transformed this room. Painting one wall a strong colour creates an instant focal point.

tips

◄ Too much of one bright colour can be overwhelming. Different spaces require different colours, depending on the lighting. Soft pastels create a soothing and relaxing atmosphere. Darker colours such as red, burgundy, navy or aubergine lend formality. Orange stimulates the appetite, and works well in a dining room.

◄ To help visually expand a room outwards, echo an interior colour on an adjoining exterior wall, especially in the living and entertaining area.

◄ For impact, stick with a two-tone colour scheme: black and white creates a dramatic feel in a kitchen or bathroom.

◄ Houses with lofty proportions can seem uninviting. Combine warm colours (reds, yellows and rust) with natural shades for balance and to create a cosy feel.

Painting practicalities

Preparing the room

Always cover furniture with plastic sheeting before you start painting. Move everything to the centre of the room, or better yet, move all the furniture to another room. Protect the floor with thick plastic or dust-sheeting. Use masking tape to cover that which you don't want to be painted. This includes everything from skirting boards and window frames, to light switches and socket outlets. Leave the tape in place until the paint is touch dry. If possible low-tack masking tape: other types will damage the surface to which it is stuck. Alternatively attach normal masking tape very carefully.

Preparing the surface

Preparation is the key to good paintwork. This process will often take longer than the actual painting, but the end results are well worth the effort. Always start with smooth, dry and clean surfaces.

Woodwork

Fill holes and cracks with filler and lightly sand; use sugar soap to remove any grease. Use a primer beforehand to seal the wood and give it a slightly rough surface so that the top coat will go on smoothly. For exteriors, remove rotted wood with a chisel and fill holes with wood filler. Sand down blisters and drip marks, wash with warm soapy water, and leave to dry.

Walls

Fill large holes and sand down to remove flaking paint and create a flat surface. Always treat mould and damp before painting.

Ceilings

Clean and rub down the ceilings where necessary.

Primers and undercoats

Primers

Primers serve two purposes: to help paint adhere to the surface, and to prevent stains and tannins from bleeding up through the paint and ruining the completed job. It is extremely important to use a primer on any wood or bare and porous surfaces, such as fresh plaster, before applying paint.

Undercoat

An undercoat is basically a more economical first coat of paint. It provides an even finish and camouflages the existing surface. However, do not use an undercoat as an alternative to a primer – it does not and will not do the same job.

Painting order

Paint your prepared room in the right order. First, cover the room with plastic sheets, and then paint the ceiling and walls. Allow to dry, then gloss-paint the wooden surfaces, i.e. the window and door frames, and finally the skirting boards.

Although a few accidental drops of emulsion paint will be easier to remove than if it were gloss paint, you are more likely to splatter emulsion paint on the wooden surfaces than you are to spill any gloss paint on the walls or ceiling. Thus this order of painting is recommended.

Painting ceilings

Start in the corner nearest to the window and use a 50 mm brush to paint around the edge all the way around the room. Roller the rest of the ceiling in 600 mm wide overlapping strips. Try to finish the job in one go to avoid a striped effect.

Working on walls

Use masking tape to protect the edgings of the wall. Then, with a 50 mm brush, paint around the ceiling, windows and door frames. Fill in the rest of the wall with a 100 mm or 150 mm wide brush or roller. Work in sections of about 1 square metre in size and try to use a continuous movement from right to left.

Ceiling secrets

For a balanced feel, floors should be darker than ceilings. Start a scheme with the floor colour and build it up from there. If you have a very high ceiling, make it appear lower by breaking up the wall with a dado rail, placed at about waist height. Paint the area below the dado rail in a darker colour, and use a lighter shade above.

You can make a lower ceiling look higher by painting the walls and ceiling the same colour. Pale, flat colours are ideal for creating this effect. You can also give a room extra height by painting vertical stripes on the walls, from floor to ceiling.

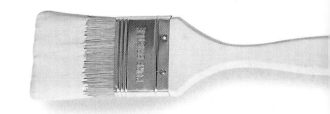

How to paint using a roller

Pour the paint into the tray to a depth of about 20 mm. First use a 50 mm paintbrush to paint a border around the wall, and to coat the corners. Use the brush to paint around light switches and plugs.

Dip the roller into the deep end of the tray. Spread the paint evenly over the roller by rolling it back and forth on the ridges of the tray ramp.

Start painting near a corner of the room, pushing the roller diagonally up the wall in 1.2 m strokes. On the second stroke, pull the roller downward then roll out the remaining paint in up-strokes. Spread paint across in vertical zigzag strokes.

Smooth surfaces by feathering. Go back over the paint and even it out, lifting the roller gradually at the end of each stroke.

How to paint using a brush

Load the brush, covering one-third of the bristle length. To remove excess paint, lift the brush straight up and slap it lightly against inside of tin. Don't drag the brush over the rim.

On large areas, apply paint with two or three overlapping diagonal brush strokes, using a large brush. Use vertical strokes to give smooth coverage.

Caring for brushes

After painting, work your brush back and forth across a newspaper to remove excess paint. When you have used oil-based paint, soak your brushes in brush cleaner then wash them out in warm (never hot) water. Store them upright, with the bristles wrapped in newspaper to preserve their shape.

When you've used water-based paint, wash brushes thoroughly with soap and water. Seperate bristles with your fingers. Leave to dry in an upright position.

Paint know-how

◀ Buy a sample pot and paint a small corner of the room – colours that look pale in the tin often appear stronger on the walls and ceiling.

◀ It is best to paint in a room temperature that is mild. Too chilly and the paint won't dry quickly enough; too hot, and it may dry irregularly.

◀ On sunny days, paint walls while they are cast in shadow, otherwise they will dry too quickly.

◀ Rub down existing paint with a dry, dark-coloured rag. If the rag collects a chalky deposit, scrub the wall with a stiff dry brush to remove loose material, then apply a stabilising solution to the surface.

◀ Use a long-nap roller with a tough nylon pile, or a large, synthetic-fibre brush to apply masonry paint. Apply the paint to the wall in vertical zigzags and fill in the gaps with vertical strokes.

◀ Because natural bristles tend to absorb water, causing them to lose their shape, select synthetic-bristle brushes for water-based paint.

◀ Paint windows and exterior doors early in the day, and paint surfaces where openings and frames meet, first.

◀ Wood should always be prepared before painting. To remove dirt and smooth out rough areas, sand the surface, then wipe with a damp cloth, and allow to dry. Use a primer on bare wood, then apply two coats of a good-quality pure acrylic paint.

◀ Prevent drips by punching four or five evenly spread holes just below the rim of the paint tin.

◀ Store paint by keeping the lid firmly on the tin when not in use. Before storing paint, clean the groove on the rim and place a layer of clingfilm over the opening to seal the tin before replacing the lid. Always store paint in its original container with the label intact so you know what it is and where it came from. Never store paint in areas that are too cold or too warm.

◀ Don't discard left-over paint – it will come in handy for touch-ups later. If only a small amount of paint is left, it won't be practical to store it in it's original container. Pour the left-over paint into an old jam jar and label it.

Flooring

Flooring can't be changed every season. Make sure you choose a floorcovering that will suit your needs. There are two basic choices – hard flooring and soft flooring. Whether you favour warm wood, cool stone, soft carpeting or natural matting, try and avoid too many different types of flooring in your home. One basic type of flooring will create unity and a feeling of spaciousness. Two layers of flooring in a room gives versatility. Use tiles as the foundation, with large rugs on top to eliminate noise and add comfort and interest.

Combinations of flooring (hard with soft or plain with patterned) are often the most eye-catching way of tackling a floor area. For instance, sanded floorboards provide a practical and attractive base, while a woollen rug introduces texture. Before you decide on a floor type, take into account the size of the room and the effect you want to create. Pale or neutral tones are good for smaller rooms as they increase the impression of light and space, while darker shades provide warmth and depth in larger rooms. Measure the room, make a note of its dimensions and any large objects within it. Take these down, make a sketch of the room, and take this along when you buy the flooring.

Hardwood floors
A wooden floor has a natural and timeless appeal and is easier to clean than other flooring. Whether stained or not, all wood should be sealed. Sealants must be reapplied from time to time.

Laminated wood flooring
Laminated wood flooring is durable, scratch-resistant, and available in a wide variety of attractive finishes. Light beech or maple is ideal for contemporary interiors, and a darker cherry or meranti will give rooms a warm exotic feel.

Mosaic
Mosaic flooring is easy to lay and can cope with a slightly uneven surface. Even so, it is still best to lay it on a flat, smooth surface. Check that all the panels are square and of the same size. An irregular panel in the middle of the floor will leave gaps. Always start at the centre of the room when laying mosaic flooring.

Concrete floors
When treated, concrete can look truly amazing. It is a very affordable heat- and scratch-resistant floor. If left untreated, however, it will soon appear dusty and dirty. Mixing coloured oxides into the cement before it is poured makes it look more glamorous. Concrete can be super glossy or diamond-ground to give it the effect of tiles. When it is cured, seal the surface with several coats of acrylic or epoxy resin to prevent it from soaking up spills. You can also use a floor paint, which will prevent dust formation and will make the floor much easier to keep clean. For a softer look, apply several coats of commercial paste wax, and give it a machine buff. Allow a newly laid concrete floor to cure for at least a month before you apply floor paint.

Vinyl flooring
Wood-effect vinyl flooring may not sound stylish, but once it is laid it looks just like the real thing. In certain areas it might even be a better choice than laminate, which can warp in damp environments such as bathrooms.

Fitted carpets
Carpets are available in wool or synthetic fibres, or in a blend that makes a good all-purpose carpet. The type of pile gives a carpet its distinct look and influences its durability.

Natural fibre floorcoverings such as sisal, seaweed or coir are extremely popular, but sisal and seaweed carpets can be a little harsh underfoot. Unless treated, sisal and coir carpets may stain and show water marks. Vacuum these floors regularly, but avoid washing and shampooing them.

tip
Wool and wool-blend carpets require moth protection. Invest in a quality underfelt to prolong the life of the carpet.

Caring for flooring
It is essential to seal stone tiles properly to prevent staining. Use very little water when cleaning, and never use household detergent, as this will strip the sealant.

Mop vinyl frequently with diluted detergent to keep it in top condition. Brush out carpet stains in the same direction as the weave, and vacuum carpets every week.

Where to use what type of flooring

Halls and stairs

Halls and stairs are heavy traffic areas. They require durable materials that can withstand a daily battering. The best choices are wood or a hard-wearing carpet. Although sisal and seaweed carpets look at home almost anywhere, they are not ideal for staircases as they can sag and become slippery over time. On wooden floors, anchor rugs firmly with anti-slip underlay.

Sitting rooms

Flooring should be comfortable and practical. Carpeting is a natural choice, because it is warm and welcoming, muffles noise and is available in so many different colours and textures. Choose neutral colours that won't force you to stick to a certain colour scheme. Rugs can be used to add interest.

Bedrooms

The bedroom is the perfect place for a thick-pile woollen carpet. Wall-to-wall fitted carpets have a luxurious quality that makes them ideal for the rooms where you relax. A neutral blends well with a variety of colour schemes. A pale carpet is pretty in a bedroom, although it is wise to choose a colour that will adapt if you change your decorating scheme. Wooden floorboards are hard-wearing and can be varnished or painted in any colour. In summer they give a cool, airy feel to a room, and for warmth in winter they can be overlaid with rugs. A blond, pale-painted or dark-stained wooden floor also works well in a bedroom. Soften the look with large rugs.

Kitchens

A kitchen floor must be durable and easy to clean. Choose tiles, stone or good-quality vinyl, in practical colours and textures that will suit the function and style of the room. For example, in a family kitchen warm vinyl, linoleum or robust terracotta tiles will be more appropriate than cold flagstone.

◂ Terracotta floor tiles are one of the most practical options for a kitchen and utility area. They are easy to clean and, with their rustic appearance, lend warmth to a room. Large tiles in a big room add to the sense of space.

◂ Brick or stone floors are ideal for heavy traffic areas. Not only are they immensely tough and durable, they also have a textural beauty that improves rather than fades with age.

◂ Marmoleum floor tiles are another good option for the kitchen. They are soft, warm to the touch and easy to clean.

tip

Flooring needn't be confined to one material – mix and match unusual combinations, such as marmoleum and stone, or show-case an area by adding borders and tiles with motifs.

Above left to right A good-quality, comfortable and attractive carpet can make a significant difference in your home. Wooden floors have a timeless appeal, while concrete floors make an affordable heat- and scratch-resistant floor.

Tiles

From marble chequerboards in grand halls, to gleaming white squares on kitchen floors and walls, tiles have always been a favourite in the home. They are beautiful, practical and hard-wearing. They come in terracotta, marble, ceramic, slate and porcelain. Tiles can create an inviting pathway to the front door. With underfloor heating, you can have warm tiles underfoot in your bathroom. A slate-covered stoep remains cool in summer. In fact, tiles are so luxurious and hard-wearing that they are perfect to use throughout your home and in the garden.

Types of tiles

There are two types of floor tiles. Soft tiles include carpet, cork, linoleum, rubber and vinyl; hard tiles include ceramic, terracotta, sandstone and quarry. Old flagstone tiles come in a subtle array of colours and are very durable. Their rugged texture echoes their natural origins and brings an outdoor element into the home. Cool in summer, they can be warmed with rugs in winter. Or, install underfloor heating elements. They are effective and not too expensive to install or run.

Choosing tiles

When choosing tiles, consider their purpose and where you want to use them. Bear in mind that laying methods vary from one type of tile to another.

Ceramic tiles

Characterised by their durability and natural beauty, these tiles are easy to clean, but can be cold to the touch and echo sound. Ideal for kitchens, bathrooms and high traffic areas such as passage ways.

Made of clay that is pressed into tiles and fired at a high temperature, they can be either hand or machine made, some with a non-slip finish. They are available in a wide variety of colours and patterns. Size and thickness can vary and tiles can be square, rectangular, hexagonal, etc. Surfaces may be glazed or unglazed.

Unglazed ceramic tiles (referred to as terracotta tiles) are highly porous and require a matt sealing treatment to prevent staining and discolouration. Usually a mix of linseed and turps is applied, as a protective coating, immediately after laying. This process darkens the colour slightly, but it prevents staining caused by household liquids or accidental spills.

tip

When purchasing unglazed tiles, ask what procedure you should follow to protect the surface.

Quarry tiles

These are made from a high-silica alumina clay that is fired to an almost glass-like hardness. They come in a range of basic colours such as buff, various reds, browns, dark blue and black. Shapes are usually square or rectangular. Impervious to water, grease and all household liquids, they are very tough, unlikely to chip and are easy to clean. They are more difficult to cut than ceramic tiles.

Terrazzo tiles

Marble chippings are set in plain or coloured cement and then ground smooth to form terrazzo tiles. Available in large slabs, they're suited to extensive floor areas, and not often used domestically, because laying and finishing small areas is expensive.

Marble

Marble is a natural material that comes in many beautiful and subtle colours. Very expensive, it is highly polished and could be slippery. Although extremely hard-wearing, marble can be damaged by using acid-based cleaners. Polish worn marble with a water-based sealer.

Natural stone

Natural stone floor slabs, such as sandstone, limestone, and granite are extremely hard-wearing and come in lovely natural hues. However, they can be cold to the touch and echo sounds. Stone varies in porosity, so when you purchase it, ask for advice about how to maintain the colour.

Slate

A dense, non-porous and extremely hard-wearing natural stone. It is generally grey with many colour variations, from blue-grey and violet-grey to grey-green tones. It looks best in square or rectangular shapes, rather than random pieces. It can have a sawn or polished finish and is available with a non-slip ridged surface.

Carpet tiles

It looks like a carpet but the benefit of these is that if a single tile is damaged or badly stained, it can easily be replaced. Use them in bedrooms, kitchens and bathrooms, or in the home office.

Vinyl tiles

These soft floor tiles come in a variety of patterns, including brick, marble and stone. It is warm underfoot, quiet and easy to keep clean. It can be slippery when wet.

How many tiles?

Before shopping, measure the size of the area in square metres (multiply the length and the width of the area). If the floor isn't exactly rectangular, you may have to break your floor into sections, measure each one, and add them together to find the total. Allow extra tiles for cuts (5 percent or 10 percent more, depending on the pattern or size of the tile you intend to use).

Right This striking combination of black and white tiles defines the kitchen work area in an open-plan space.

Tile makeover

Give your existing tiles a makeover with a new coat of paint. Bear in mind that you'll lose contrasting grouting.

◄ Ensure that tiles are dry and free of dirt, grease and limescale.
◄ Using a synthetic brush or roller, apply a thin, even coat of tile primer over the tile, the edges and grouting and leave to dry for eight hours. If the tiles have a raised effect, work the primer into the spaces. Apply a second coat, if required.
◄ Once dry, sand the surface very lightly to remove any dirty marks; dust clean.
◄ Apply two coats of tile or gloss paint in your chosen colour.

Many people wrongly assume that tiling a wall or floor is something only professionals should do. Make sure you have the right tools and materials for the job, then follow these easy steps, and see just how simple a tiling job can be.

create the look

you will need:

- ✓ tiles
- ✓ tape measure
- ✓ chalk
- ✓ tile adhesive
- ✓ notched spreader
- ✓ grout
- ✓ damp sponge
- ✓ dry lint-free cloth
- ✓ tile spacer
- ✓ spirit level
- ✓ dowel

how to:

1. Set out the tiles. In a room that has a regular shape, find the centre of the floor by linking the midpoints of the opposite pairs of walls with string lines. In a room that has an irregular shape, place string lines so that they avoid obstructions, then link the midpoints of opposite pairs of strings to find the centre of the room.

2. Start in the centre. Dry-lay rows of tiles out towards the walls in each direction to see how many whole tiles will fit in and to check the fit. Allow for the thickness of the joints. Move the rows slightly to improve the fit if necessary, and then mark the string lines on the floor with chalk.

3. Lay the tiles. Using the spreader, spread some adhesive on the floor. Lay the border tiles first, then start the diagonal tile work in the centre of the floor. Use tile spacers to ensure even gaps between the tiles. Use a straight edge to check that all the tiles are horizontal and level.

4. Use a soft sponge to clean the tiles off while working – don't allow the adhesive to dry on the tiles. Allow 24 hours for the tiles to set.

5. Grouting. Before grouting, remove any adhesive and loose matter between the tiles. Use a squeegee to spread the grout over the tiles and fill the joins. Wipe off the surplus grout with a damp sponge before it dries. Smooth the grout with a dowel. Allow the grout to set in each joint for about five to 10 minutes.

6. Wash the tiles with a sponge and water to clean off excess grout.

7. Allow the grout to dry before sealing the tiles. This should take between three days and a week.

cutting tiles

Tile cutters can be hired from a hardware store. Mark the tile where you want to cut it, then place the tile in the tile cutter, and draw the cutting wheel firmly and smoothly across the surface (once) to make a clean scratch across the tile. Press down firmly with the tile cutter handle. The tile will break cleanly in two parts along the scratch. Use tile nippers to make contour cuts, taking small bites from the edge of the tile. If the edge is somewhat jagged, use a rubbing stone or another tile to smooth it out.

Carpeting

Carpeting softens the overall feel of a room and forms a back-drop for everything therein. It also provides texture, sound absorption and colour. It should contribute to creating a balanced room; if it draws too much attention, the balance might be disturbed.

A safe way to choose the colour of wall-to-wall carpeting is to select a similar shade to that of the wall – just a hint darker or lighter, depending on the intensity of the colour that was used. Match various carpet samples with your choice of paint and upholstery. The carpet shade should never be the dominant colour in a room.

Other factors to consider include climate, traffic and how much daylight the room receives. In cooler climates, warm, cosy carpets are the obvious choice. In humid and hot climates, opt for natural fibres. Heavy traffic areas will need durable, practical, and washable carpeting.

The more luxurious types of carpeting are suitable for bedrooms and areas with little traffic. Use lighter colours in rooms that don't get much natural light; use darker colours in rooms that receive more light – the carpet will appear lighter. When choosing a carpet, a very important factor to consider is the fibre from which it is made.

Natural fibres

Wool

Wool is strong, dyes easily and won't show furniture imprints due to the resilience of the fibre. It is fire resistant and has natural insulation properties. It does not trap dirt or dust easily, but needs to be protected against insects and spills.

Sisal

Sisal is nonstatic, won't trap dirt or dust and, if woven correctly, will retain its shape for years. Slight irregularities in thickness and colour occur. It can be dyed in a vast array of colours.

Jute

Slight matting can occur in high-traffic areas and adding separate padding is recommended to improve the carpet's wear and resilience. Jute is nonstatic and won't trap dirt and dust.

Seagrass

Seagrass is smooth to the touch, has a low, natural sheen, is durable, nonstatic and won't matt easily.

Coir

Coir is extremely resilient, with carpets retaining their shape for years if woven correctly. Little or no matting occurs and the fibres are bleached and dyed in a vast array of colours.

Synthetic fibres

Nylon

Designed to resist matting and static, soiling and staining, it is versatile and can easily be dyed. Nylon does not fade easily.

Polyester

It's less expensive than other synthetics, but not very durable. Suitable for low-traffic areas such as bedrooms, polyester has a soft feel, is nonstatic and does not absorb moisture, making it less prone to staining.

Polypropylene

Moisture, stain and fade resistant; it is non-allergenic and mould and mildew resistant. Best suited to loop-style carpets, it can be used for both in- and outdoors. It is not as resistant to matting and crushing as nylon fibres.

How to determine quality

Density is the measure of how tightly together the fibres are attached to the backing. The closer the fibres are, the less wear there is on individual fibres and therefore the longer it will last. To test for density, push your hand against the fibres, forcing them to one side. The less visible the backing, the denser the carpet. Another way of testing is to run your fingers through the fibres, pushing down towards the backing. In a better quality carpet, little backing will be felt. Pay attention to the strength of the tuft bind – it must be properly attached to the backing to prevent fibres from coming loose and deteriorating. In cut pile carpet styles, the tightness of the twist in certain styles is also important – the tighter the twist, the better the quality, as it will resist matting and crushing. A warranty is also telling. Usually the longer the warranty, the better the quality. Top quality carpeting can have up to a 25-year warranty.

Practical matters

Lower, densely packed cut pile or loop-style carpets are the most durable and hard-wearing options. They are easy to clean and suitable for high-traffic areas such as passage ways, family and children's rooms.

Luxury living

Luxurious carpets absorb more sound and are comfortable and soft underfoot, but they can be difficult to keep clean and are easily trampled. Best reserved for low-traffic areas.

Formal living

Carpets with a smooth, cut pile surface are suitable for a formal or semi-formal look. Some cut pile carpets, especially ones with a longer pile, tend to show footprints.

Relaxed living

Loop-style carpeting, as well as rustic-woven natural fibre carpets all have a more informal look and are suitable for family rooms and general living. These do not show footprints, and various textured effects are available in a variety of colours.

Keep in mind

◀ Plain carpeting, especially in lighter colours, shows up dirt quite easily, whereas patterned carpeting does not.

◀ A larger expanse of carpet will always appear darker than the shop sample, since the colour is intensified by size. Counter-balance this by choosing a sample that is a tone lighter.

◀ If patterned carpeting is preferred, keep in mind that a heavy pattern, especially one with variously coloured designs, will make a room appear smaller. Opt for smaller patterns in lighter colours if the area to be carpeted is fairly small.

Rugs

Rugs add colour and interest and make great focal points. A rug can be used as a starting point for decorating – especially if it has striking colours or a pattern that can be copied or com-plemented. Rugs can also be used to divide an expanse of

flooring into more intimate areas, by grouping chairs and tables on or around them. All the pieces of furniture must either fit comfortably on the carpet or be completely off it.

Good advice

◀ If curling or waving of a rug occurs, roll the corners back down and weigh down overnight with heavy books.

◀ Renting and stuck with terrible carpeting in your room? Start by having it professionally steam-cleaned or washed to improve the appearance. Alternatively, you could hide it under a couple of matching loose rugs.

◀ Save by having room-sized carpets made up. Have the carpeting edged and mitred neatly to match the shape of the room or have it cut about 30 to 40 cm smaller all around to leave a neat edge of the flooring beneath showing all around. You can take these with you when you move.

Right Use loose rugs to make rooms with wooden or tiled floors appear warmer and more inviting.

Storage

Display and storage space is needed in absolutely every room in the house. Before making hasty decisions, consider all the practical requirements. Ask yourself the following:

◄ What do I need to store?
◄ What do I need to organise?
◄ What do I need to keep safe and secure?
◄ Which items do I want to display?
◄ What do I want to conceal?

Value of storage space

No home can have too much storage space. Having adequate storage in your home will increase the value of your investment. Storage space is particularly important in the kitchen and bedrooms. You can never have enough built-in cupboards, shelving and open display units.

Consider how much storage space you need, then double it. Clutter has an amazing habit of reproducing itself when you're not looking. One day you have beautiful, clutter-free shelves; the next day you can't seem to find your shelves!

Kitchen storage

Try and keep each item close to where it is most often needed. Store crockery in built-in units, open shelves or traditional dressers. Open shelves are easily accessible and attractive for displaying crockery, but pieces are exposed to grease and dust. Place them away from steamy areas such as the stove and sink.

Most people prefer cutlery in a cutlery basket. Otherwise, pack away in drawers with special tiered fittings, or in a standard cutlery tray with separate grooves for each piece.

For perishable food, the fridge and freezer, or a combination of the two, are an absolute must-have storage unit in the kitchen. A breadbin and vegetable basket are also useful.

Divide your groceries into jars, tins, baking ingredients and dry goods. A pantry with shelving offers ideal storage space.

Store pots and pans as close to the stove, oven, microwave or hob as possible.

Storage options include open shelves, an under-hob rack, a cupboard above the oven, or a island working unit on wheels that can serve as storage space as well as a worktop. Maximise space by hanging saucepans, kitchen utensils and baskets from an old-fashioned airer.

Living area

The living room must be comfortable and convenient, and at the same time should function as the relaxation room for watching television, listening to music or reading a book.

Keep the room clutter-free by allowing plenty of storage space. A coffee table is often the central furniture item in this room. Keep the surface clutter-free by choosing one with drawers or a lower shelf in which to store items. You can display favourite objects such as a book collection, vases, shells, and so on in shelves, recessed alcoves, or built-in cabinets, and hide your television, DVD-player, music system and video-recorder in a free-standing TV cabinet with closing doors to create a feeling of space and order. Store video cassettes and other hobby items in attractive wicker baskets or wooden boxes on open shelves.

For a romantic feel, opt for an elegant armoire with interior shelving to suit your storage needs. To make a strong visual statement, opt for a CD rack to store your music collection. Either wall-mounted or free-standing, they are a 21st-century necessity and can be made from wood or metal. A sideboard is useful to house your best crockery and glassware.

tip
Store books upright because stacking may damage them. Make sure they are not too crowded or too loosely packed.

Opposite Clever use of available space under the desk and on the walls, ensures that a usually cluttered study area remains neat and tidy.

Utilise wall space:

◄ Maximise floor space by using suspended shelving.

◄ A bookshelf or tallboy can add character to a bare wall and can also be a great place to display decorative items, such as picture frames and flowers.

◄ The mantel over your fireplace is the perfect spot for small items. Keep other items in decorative boxes rather than cluttering up the entire shelf.

◄ Think about installing box recesses into the walls. These provide great storage space and look stylish.

◄ If you have an alcove (and a tight budget), opt for shelves in scaffolding or reclaimed wood. Cut the desired length and paint in the colour of your choice or leave bare.

Focus on detail

Keep newspapers and magazines neat and tidy and store them in a magazine rack that co-ordinates with your interior.

There are many different styles of decorative and contemporary storage boxes on the market, but why not decorate your own by covering old shoeboxes with pretty paper that blends well with the scheme of your room?

Organise your home with natural woven baskets. They are hard-wearing, practical and look great. Keep paperwork in woven stacking trays, labelled with luggage tags.

Keep household bills and receipts in pretty envelopes, pinned onto a board painted and covered in fabric.

Bathroom

Create a tranquil and serene space, using a combination of open and closed storage to display certain items, and conceal others. Opt for a decorative shelf to display attractive toiletries, a bath rack for bath accessories and a corner unit to house shower accessories.

If your bathroom is big enough, choose a freestanding cupboard with shelves on which you can store towels, toiletries and toilet paper.

A wall-mounted cabinet or recessed shelves, that take up no extra space, are good choices for smaller bathrooms. A mobile trolley is also an option.

Invest in a laundry basket for every bedroom, rather than having only one in the bathroom. This will prevent dirty laundry from piling up on the bathroom and bedroom floors.

tip

Keep towel rails within easy reach of the bath, shower or basin. Always position the medicine cabinet out of reach of small children.

Bedroom

There is a definite air of ordered indulgence in the bedroom. Reduce clutter with plenty of custom-built cupboards for storage. Allow for a variety of storage systems such as shelving, drawers and ample hanging space.

Conceal your books, magazines and other bedside necessities inside bedside tables or built-in shelves at the head of the bed. Keep extra blankets in a kist, chest or trunk, that can double up as seating, at the foot of the bed. Wicker baskets and pull-out bags are great alternatives for storing out-of-season goodies.

tips
‹ The ideal height for a bedside table is approximately level with the top of your mattress.
‹ Fit wall-mounted lights or reading lamps to the headboard to save space on a small bedside table.

Children's rooms
This room needs to be adaptable. It should provide fun spaces for playing, as well as being a restful place in which to sleep. To make it more flexible, put anything you can on casters, for example, wooden drawers for under the bed (to stack sports equipment) or a large box or a basket for toys. Chrome hooks on the wall can be used to hang all sorts of items – from a favourite T-shirt to sneakers and assorted toys.

Opposite, and above, left and right Look for baskets, chests and any other clever storage units that will keep clutter out of sight, but still ensure easy access to the items you have stored.

Insulation and heating

Insulation

It is essential to ensure that your home is well insulated. It will keep your home warm in winter and cool in summer. In doing away with the need for heaters and air conditioners, you could save up to R1 200 a year on electricity bills.

In midsummer, the concentrated effect of the sun's rays on roofing creates a heat trap between the roof and the ceiling. Without insulation, the ceiling will transmit that heat to the rooms below, creating temperatures that are often uncomfortably high. In winter, the reverse happens. Heat rises and easily passes through a ceiling that is not insulated. As the heat escapes through the ceiling, cold air is sucked in to take its place.

Aerolite, a pink mineral fibre, is the most popular insulation material on the market. It is made of pure-spun fibreglass, bonded together with an inert thermo-setting resin. The result is a strong, resilient, easily handled, thick blanket with millions of tiny pockets of air around the fibres. Fibreglass does not conduct electricity, so exposed wiring will not short-circuit and set it alight. Pink fibreglass is lightweight, rot-proof and odourless, and will not be eaten by vermin. It assists in reducing sound transmission. It can be purchased in 400 mm and 1 200 mm wide rolls, in thicknesses of 50 mm, 75 mm or 100 mm. The thicker the material, the better the insulation. It is also fire resistant and noncombustible.

Underfloor heating

Underfloor heating provides the main source of heat. If you consider having underfloor heating installed, bear in mind that you will lose around 8 cm from the height of the room once the hot-water pipes, insulation, concrete screed and flooring have been laid.

Fireplaces

Nothing beats stretching out in front of a cosy fire in winter. A fireplace creates a glowing and attractive focal point to any room, and is a surprisingly economical way to keep warm.

In older homes, many fireplaces were removed and chimneys sealed. Luckily, both can be reinstated, although the openings may need to be adjusted to fit the fireplace. This can be a messy, labour-intensive job, so best you call in a builder.

New fireplaces come in a range of styles to suit almost any décor, and tend to be much more efficient than older, fitted fireplaces. Shop around for something to suit your style and your pocket.

Before you start installing the fireplace, check that the hearth is level and the fireback (the concrete slab surrounding the opening) is in good order. If it isn't, or doesn't fit the new surrounds, call in an expert to assist you.

Wiring and electricity

Most households cannot do without electricity, but few of us know exactly how it works. In fact, few of us know even the basics, such as how to wire a plug. Electricity is potentially dangerous and even this small task, if done incorrectly, could cause a fire. Special care must be taken in bathrooms and near kitchen sinks, as electricity and water are a deadly combination.

Planning plug points

Plan a sufficient number of plug points per room. In older homes most rooms have only one plug point. Draw up a plan and mark the most important plugs that you will need in a specific room. In the living room, for instance, you will need at least two to three plug points for a standing lamp, a music system, television and a table lamp. Ask an electrician to install more plug points, if necessary.

Moving electrical boards

In many older homes the unsightly electrical distribution box is right in the entrance hallway or somewhere in the kitchen. If you would like to move the box to another location (you can hide it in a cupboard where it is still easily accessible), an electrician must do the job. This can be extremely costly, depending on the location of the wiring system. You will, probably, have to inform your local municipality as well.

tips

The most important rule when working with electricity is safety. Always turn off the mains switch before doing any electrical work in the home. Then use a circuit tester to check that the switch, socket or light is dead.
Extension leads are not intended as fixed features. Use them only when there is no easy access to a plug point.

---

wiring DIY

wiring a plug

Strip the ends of the flex with wire strippers, and remove about 6 mm of insulation material from each of the three cores. Twist the exposed wires in each core. Open the plug by undoing the screws on the casing. Push each set of wires through the hole in the correct terminal. No bare wire should be visible. Screw the top of each terminal down securely. Replace the plug cover.

installing a dimmer switch

Switch off the power at the distribution board. Unscrew and remove the existing faceplate from the wall. Unscrew the inner plate and remove the switch unit. Use an insulated screwdriver to take the wiring out of the terminals. Clean any dirt out of the cavity behind the old box. Screw the new box into place and connect the wiring to the terminals. Place the faceplate over the switch and the knob, and screw into place over the box. Replacing a socket is the same as fitting a dimmer switch.

tip

The way wiring is connected within plugs is universal. The earth terminal is in the centre at the top of the plug. Neutral is on the left and the live core is joined to the terminal on the right. This is usually indicated with the letters N, E and L, or by colour – the live core being brown, neutral blue and the earth core yellow and green.

Opposite A fireplace creates a glowing and attractive focal point in any room, and is an economical way to keep warm.

A house is a substantial investment, therefore it is vitally important that you keep it well maintained. Make regular inspections and correct any problems as soon as they arise. When maintaining your home, prevention is better (and will cost you much less) than cure.

Regular maintenance

Home maintenance should not only be carried out when there is a crisis. Your first maintenance check should be done before you start any decorating projects. Although it's great fun spending spare cash on new bedding or funky kitchen appliances, it is essential that you put this extra money towards the routine maintenance of your home. A regular and modest investment will result in a long-term saving of both time and money. You will be able to prevent, for example, major structural problems and damage before it occurs, and avoid being faced with huge bills that you are unable to pay.

A regular home maintenance programme should include the inspection of the house and all its fixtures and structures, as well as more routine inspections, such as making sure that no drains are blocked. Keep a record of all inspections and maintenance. This will allow you to become familiar with your house and your property, making it easy for you to identify problem areas and those repairs that carry priority status. Records of inspections will enable you to plan for financial assistance, should you need any, and will prove useful should you ever decide to sell your house.

Continuous inspections and repairs will lessen the effects of everyday wear and tear, and in so doing, prolong the lifespan of your house, and your pocket! You may still need to undertake one or two major maintenance jobs every few years (such as repainting the interior and exterior of your home), but in the long run, regular home maintenace will only count in your favour.

When doing a maintenance inspection, work from top to bottom. Include everything from the roof and gutters to the interior walls and the floor covering.

Tackle the roof

Acrophobia is no excuse for not inspecting your roof. Use binoculars if you're afraid of heights and do the inspection from the ground. Be on the look-out for loose, worn, damaged or missing shingles; look for blisters or cracks on flat roofs. The roof must be well clear of any branches; the gutters should be debris-free. Check for loose or rusty chimney areas, and that the chimney itself is clear. Check for loose wires on roof-mounted equipment. If you notice trouble spots, call an expert. Keep safety in mind at all times and never attempt an inspection on the roof unless there is someone on the ground to assist you.

Inspect the roof for cracks, splits or tears that may cause leaking. Flat roofs are particularly susceptible to blistering and splitting; check damaged areas for possible leakage.

Plain roof tiles that are damaged or missing, and slate shingles that have slipped out of place, are often the source of a leak.

Inspect skylights, vents and chimneys. Cement mortar inside the chimney should not be brittle and come loose when lightly scraped.

Check all areas where metal meets brick, and wood meets brick or metal. These surfaces expand and contract at different rates, and thus tend to pull away from each other. Inspect all seals. A loose seal might indicate a leak.

If all else fails, try to locate the leak from inside the house. Use a strong flashlight, and follow the leak to its source.

Guttering

Broken, clogged or cracked gutters can cause serious water damage. Wait for a rainy day to do a thorough inspection, and check for leaks and sections where water is overflowing. Inspect and clear your guttering of any debris at least once a year. If there are trees near the house, remove leaves on a regular basis. Or, simply prevent blockages by inserting plastic (or wire) mesh and leaf guards. Use a garden hose to test the flow of water through each gutter.

Walls, windows and doors

Areas most exposed to the elements need regular inspection and maintenance. Inspect the exterior walls and look for problems such as peeling or fading paint, cracks and signs of damp.

Door hinges, and hardware on windows should be checked for signs of rust and corrosion. Also check screens and railings around the stoep.

Rotting window frames not only let in cold, but increase the risk of damp, which in turn spells trouble for interior walls and floors. If you regularly paint the window frames as part of your maintenance programme, you should notice problems like these in good time.

Foundations

Termites and water pose the greatest threat to foundations. Look for signs of damage or deterioration of wood, or the presence of earthen tubes (built by termites) along foundation walls or exposed pipes. Problem drains, damaged gutters and factors such as a high water table can cause water damage. Look for water stains and damp spots. If water damage has occurred you may detect a hint of mildew in the air.

Moisture matters

Excessive moisture can be caused by and lead to a number of problems in the home, the most common of which is damp. Moisture from waterlogged ground can seep into the home via

Left If you're afraid of heights, make an initial roof inspection from inside the attic. Let an expert do the nerve-wrecking outside inspection, or inspect the roof on safe ground, using binoculars

the foundation, causing damp spots. Damp can also be caused by leaking roofs and gutters, faulty windows and doors, or incorrectly laid concrete or brickwork. If left untreated it will, over time, cause extensive damage to and the deterioration of both the interior and the exterior of your home.

The first signs to look for are rotten wood, discoloured brick-work, or paint that has lifted and peeled. When treating damp, the first and most important thing to do is to find the source of the problem. Simply treating or replacing rotten wood, for example, is a quick and easy solution, but it's not a permanent one. And before you know it, the wood will be rotten again.

Interior moisture damage

Moisture doesn't penetrate the home from outside alone. Inside your home, you contribute to the build-up of moisture by bathing, cooking, washing and even breathing.

In bathrooms and kitchens, excessive moisture can cause tiles to lift. Be on the look-out for this; make sure the floor under-neath is not rotten. Ensure that there is adequate ventilation and possibly even an extractor fan through which moisture build-up can escape. Inspect the walls during the day, especially where cracks in walls and under windows allow water access. Dark patches on the walls or under the windows, are usually an indication of water damage.

Also look for dry rot, which is characterised by a white growth resembling cotton wool. If dry rot is present, you have a serious problem. It is a rather extreme form of decay and, to prevent it from spreading, will need urgent treatment. Dry rot is most commonly found under floors, behind skirting boards and underneath paint. It thrives in damp and poorly ventilated areas and can spread far wider than the timber where it starts. Do not let this happen.

Inspect the insulation and make sure it isn't wet. Prevent moisture-related problems by ensuring that your home is properly sealed off from the outside. Just enough fresh air should be let in, and there should be just enough ventilation for moisture build-up to escape.

If painted woodwork, doors and panelling are discoloured or stained by water from inside walls or ceilings, they can usually be restored with a moderate amount of work. If the painted surface is blistered or the paint is peeling, it may be necessary to strip the paint down to the wood for a smooth finish. Many types of paint and varnish removers are available. Follow the manufacturer's instructions carefully when you use paint removers, and don't try any shortcuts.

If painted wood isn't damaged, but has become dulled, discoloured or stained, clean the surface thoroughly, sand it lightly and apply an enamel undercoat. Allow the undercoat to dry completely, then sand lightly with very fine sandpaper. Wipe clean and apply enamel paint.

Minor damage to finished natural wood may be repaired with a light sanding, followed by a coat of gloss or semi-gloss clear varnish. For extensive damage, remove the finish, sand the wood until smooth, and refinish.

If water has caused plaster to swell and crumble, or if sections have collapsed, new plaster may be needed. If your home has specific trouble areas, you may need to check them several times a year.

To treat dry rot in wooden floors, first dry out the entire house; use heaters if necessary. Remove every bit of rotten wood, including all wood, at least 400 mm from the last evidence of rot. Where the drying out may be delayed, for example in brickwork or inaccessible areas, treat the surface with an appropriate preservative after removal of plaster and other affected surfaces. Replace all rotten timber with treated timber, and also treat all remaining timber with at least two coats of preservative. Make sure all areas that could possibly be affected are well ventilated.

Replace damaged floorboards, but keep in mind that the new boards will stand out from the old ones; if quite a few floorboards are broken or chipped, consider replacing the whole lot. Use the width and length of the old boards as a guide when you look for replacements.

Check all the joists for damage and ensure they are level before you start replacing odd floorboards. Make sure that any damaged sections are replaced, and weakened sections are strengthened, before you start any other work.

Buried treasure

Beneath the old and slightly worn carpets of your new home, there may lie a hidden treasure just waiting to be discovered. Before planning new wall-to-wall carpets, make sure the old carpets aren't concealing a charming wooden floor. Timber flooring is one of the most versatile floorcoverings and will suit just about any style of home.

Old floorboards are easily restored to their former glory. All you need to do is sand them smooth and apply a healthy coat of varnish. You could also lay an entirely new timber floor, and finish it with stains and varnish to bring out the natural splendour of the wood.

Providing character and a certain old-worldly charm, wooden floors are absolutely wonderful to have in a home. If you've bought a home with wooden floors, or are interested in one, do check for beetle infestation. In South Africa you are required, by law, to receive a certificate from the seller stating that the wooden floors and other areas are beetle-free. For your own peace of mind, do an on-site inspection and look for tell-tale signs such as small holes in the wood; the wood will also be porous and prone to breaking.

Keep it regular

Apart from the structure of the house, you should regularly inspect other areas such as the electrical system, plumbing (look out for dripping taps or toilets) and the walls inside your house. Also make sure the taps don't leak, and that there is adequate water pressure. Flush the toilets. And look for water leaks against the walls and ceiling.

When repairing your home, it is extremely important that you do every job thoroughly and precisely according to instructions. Don't try any shortcuts or give in to the temptation of doing improvements that you think will be more fun. Do the necessary repairs first! There's little point in decorating your home, only to have it fall apart within a year, because you haven't properly maintained its structure.

Repairs often take longer and cost more than anticipated, so do not to commit to other expensive projects before the basic problems have been corrected.

Mortgage bond tip

When building, do not sign consent-to-progress payments before you are satisfied with the work done; obtain expert advice if necessary. If you are buying a renovated or older home, it would be wise to get an expert to inspect the building.

personal inspection check list

◄ **Leaks**: look for interior and exterior evidence of leaks. Check all ceilings and areas around the windows, as well as skylights, if applicable.

◄ **Foundation**: look for any obvious cracks or any clear signs that the foundation has shifted.

◄ **Roof**: is it old or new? What is the general condition of the roof? Apart from looking out for loose tiles, also check that the top of the roof hasn't imploded, an indication of possible structural or ceiling damage.

◄ **Plumbing**: listen for any abnormal sounds when using taps; make sure all the bathroom plumbing works efficiently.

◄ **Electrical**: switch everything on and off; check for obvious problems.

◄ **Quality of finishes**: check the general quality of the finishes – everything from taps, tiles and burglar bars, to carpets and light fittings.

◄ **Exterior**: will you need to give the house a new coat of paint, or do some urgent repairs soon after moving in?

◄ **Newly painted interior**: if the house has recently been painted, make sure that the new coat of paint hasn't been used only to cover up cracks in walls, which will reappear in a few weeks' time.

◄ **Ceilings**: look for water damage and stains, cracks and sagging.

◄ **Drains and gutters**: check for blockages.

Space is a valuable commodity in any home, whether it be a small batchelor's flat or a modest three-bedroomed house. To make the most of every room in your home, it is important that you maximise space and utilise it to its full potential. There are a number of simple and easy ways in which you can achieve this.

maximising space

With the ever-increasing cost of building materials, new homes are becoming more compact, and the rooms within them radically smaller. As a result, living spaces need to be planned with more care, both visually and in terms of practicality. Every space needs to be a dual purpose area, and every item of furniture needs to be multi-functional.

Storage units are now designed in modules that can accommodate entertainment systems and books; they come with flap-down (retractable) work surfaces that can be used as a desk, dining table or sewing surface, and they have enough space for just about any item that needs to be stored or displayed.

Choose smaller seating units, and coffee tables with storage facilities. Use a room divider to create a dual-purpose space. Maximise your wall space by installing floor-to-ceiling shelves, or maximise floor space by making use of built-in furniture, such as a window seat that also doubles as a storage unit.

Colour and space

Colour is the simplest and most effective tool with which to change a room cosmetically. If used to good effect, the right combination of colour, texture and pattern can dramatically transform a room, making the smallest look larger than life, or the most spacious warm and cosy.

Use the same colour (preferably pale) for the walls, floor and large pieces of furniture. In so doing, the most confined area will appear lighter and airier, and bulky objects like settees, armchairs and beds will blend with the background. You can alleviate dullness by using the same colours in different textures,

and by adding accent colour with accessories, such as plants, scatter cushions, pictures, books and ornaments. Use the colour wheel to select the right tones, and make any decorating scheme work for you. The secret to creating a stylish home and to maximising space is in choosing just the right depth of colour for the effect that you wish to create.

The right colour

Depending on the hue and the way in which it is used, colour can have a dramatic effect on the proportions of a room. In general, warm colours, such as red, orange, yellow and brown can make a room appear more intimate and cosy. These colours are also known as advancing colours, because in addition to making a room appear more warm and welcoming, they can also make wall and ceiling surfaces appear closer to the viewer than they actually are, thus making a room seem smaller than it is in reality.

On the other side of the colour wheel, the cooler hues create the opposite visual effect. Also known as receding colours, they can make a room appear larger than it actually is, and give a cool and light feel to a room. Paler colours have the same visual effect and therefore the ideal way to create the illusion of space is to use these two in combination with each other.

Pale colours that have a soft, muted feel are ideal for creating a gentle and restful atmosphere in any room within the house. Choose from a variety of colours, such as shades of grey or cream, perhaps a duck-egg blue, or taupe, or maybe faded pink. Lift them with strong contrasting colours from the opposite side of the colour wheel, such as red or purple, aubergine or pure white. Using one colour throughout will create a feeling of space and tranquillity; varying shades of the same colour will lend dimension to your colour scheme. Black or a dark wood tint is useful to liven up the other colours. To ensure a feeling of spaciousness in any room, painted any colour, make sure that your ceiling is always a shade lighter than the walls.

Left This large room, shared by two teenagers, has been divided with RhinoWall to give each occupant a measure of privacy.
Opposite Simple, sheer curtains create a spacious feel by letting in the maximum amount of light.

Above A floating shelf with a streamlined design keeps the floor area clean, and creates the illusion of space. The horizontal line of the shelving also makes a the short wall look much longer, increasing the perceived dimensions of the room.

Delightful

Good lighting is essential for any room to feel spacious. Find the perfect combination of natural and artificial light to make the most of the space you have.

Magical mirrors

Mirrors have the dual function of reflecting light and creating the illusion of more space. A large mirror or a mirrored wall surface can double the visual size of an area. If you're using more than one mirror be sure to place them all at the same height, as a sea of mirrors can be very disorientating. Before buying an expensive cut-glass mirror, make sure that it will be able to fit through doors, up stairways and into lifts, because there is no way you can bend it!

Wonderful windows

Open the windows and let the sun shine in! You can replace small windows with larger ones, and heavy window treatments with window film or glass blocks for privacy.

Installing skylights is another option that works really well. Skylights allow maximum natural light into a room, because the aspect of your house does not greatly affect the amount of sunlight the skylight receives.

Clear away clutter

Remove all clutter on the floor and on countertops, and be ruthless! There's little point in spending a small fortune on redecorating if the whole effect is just going to disappear underneath the same old piles of junk. Find better ways to make use of that space. Hide anything that isn't essential, or throw it away. Find a modest storage unit that suits the room well and use it specifically for daily clutter-control clean-ups.

Buy practical furniture with built-in storage. Invest in a dual-purpose coffee table that can also be used as a chest of drawers for games or magazines.

Expand outdoors

Expand your living room by using the same colours and style in which it was decorated, to decorate your patio, stoep, balcony or veranda. You will not only extend and maximise your living space, but also have a much larger area in which to entertain.

quick ways to create space in your home

If your home feels cramped and you can't afford to expand, try using any of these simple, yet very effective, space-saving tips.

‹ Keep things simple and open. To create the illusion of more space, reduce the number of visual elements by specifying simple cabinet styles. Remove cabinet doors to avoid a boxed-in feeling.

‹ Eliminate clutter. The less clutter, the bigger and more open a room will feel and look.

‹ Bring in as much natural light as possible. Light makes a room much more appealing, and easy to relax or work in. Apply window film for privacy.

‹ Opt for a neutral or pastel colour scheme, and limit the number of colours and patterns you use.

‹ If you can, leave at least one wall in a room unit-free.

‹ Ask a kitchen design expert for advice on having drawers built into your unit plinths.

‹ In a small room, the use of too many colours will only emphasise the room's lack of space. Restrict your palette to a maximum of three colours.

‹ Consider having the edges of work surfaces curved – it will cost a bit more, but will really make a big difference in your kitchen.

If you've tried the space-saving tips and your home still feels that tiny little bit too small, try some of these space-creating ideas in which colour, accessories and soft furnishings are used to help stretch a room without changing its structure.

‹ Use the palest colours and limit the hues of accessories, or stick to one basic colour and vary the textures of fabrics and finishes.

‹ Paint ceilings and walls in the same light colour to create the illusion of space. The floor should be a light or natural colour from wall to wall, without any loose rugs (particularly in a small room).

‹ Create a three-dimensional effect by using patterns of colours, against a white background.

‹ Go for geometric, directional or diagonal lines on a floor or wall. Dark colours on a light background work particularly well to give depth as well as create perspective.

‹ Create the illusion of space by placing objects in front of a large mirror, or set a table with a lamp, or place a plant in front of the hinges of a screen.

‹ Use blinds in combination with curtains, and leave vertical louvre blinds half-open.

‹ Short walls can be made to look longer by introducing strong horizontal lines of shelving.

‹ Visually expand space by mounting mirrors on a wall, door or on cupboards. Plate glass is expensive, so economise by using mirror tiles, pre-cut mirrors or mirrored laminate.

‹ Avoid cramming. Keep furniture to a minimum and, preferably, simple and streamlined in design. Where possible, have furniture built in along walls.

‹ You can gain extra storage space in hallways with built-in shelving and cupboards. Do the same with recesses and alcoves, particularly on either side of a chimney breast.

‹ Build a comfortable seat under a window, with foam cushions on top and storage space – neatly concealed behind sliding doors – underneath.

‹ If floor space has to be divided, do it with open-work screens of bamboo or wooden trellis, or even with tall plants.

‹ Cane, rattan or wicker furniture is light and gives a feeling of spaciousness.

‹ For tables, use clear glass or translucent Perspex or Plexiglass, where possible.

Breaking out a wall

Breaking out the wall that divides two rooms can create a much larger single room with two separate functions. For example, in the house depicted in the floorplan below, the wall between the dining room and the kitchen was removed to allow the light from the living area to reach the kitchen. It also provides an easy flow between the kitchen, the living area and the outdoor courtyard. This is the ideal lay-out when it comes to entertaining and playing hostess to many guests.

Removing the wall that separated the lounge from the entrance hall not only makes the lounge appear much larger, but it also allows the beautiful fireplace to draw your eye instantly as you walk through the front door.

A house is a finely balanced structure and each part or section thereof is dependent on the other. The removal of one part will have a direct influence and effect on all the other parts of the structure.

Load-bearing walls are usually two bricks deep, and if the wall is supporting one, i.e. it supports the roof or an upper-level room, it may not be removed entirely. Also, you would have to install a concrete beam or lintel to replace the wall. In this instance, it would be best to obtain advice from a structural engineer. A structural engineer will be able to determine the load capacity of the wall you would like to remove, as well as what the consequences, if any, of its removal will be. He or she may also be able to provide you with possible alternatives.

When removing an internal brick wall, bear in mind that it will leave a gap in the floor where the wall was (walls are built up from the foundation, which is below floor level) and it may be necessary to replace all the floorboards or the whole carpet in a newly created room.

Municipal laws could dictate that you may not remove internal walls, or that you need permission from a structural engineer to go ahead with the job. It is best to check with your local council's building or planning department first.

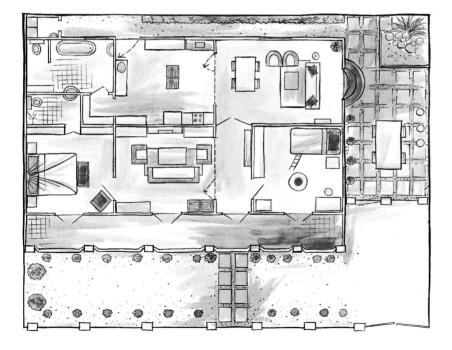

Left The red lines on this floorplan indicate where internal walls were removed in the Dreamhouse.

Our house: THE LAY-OUT

before

The kitchen was dark, dull and dated, with two doors leading directly from the kitchen to the two separate bathrooms. The living room in the south-east corner of the house received very little natural light and was thus dark and cold. It was also cut off from the rest of the house, and in particular, from the kitchen. We would never have imagined how simple and easy it was going to be to transform these rooms into more functional areas that were lighter, brighter, as well as all connected.

after

We removed the wall between the kitchen and living area to make the rooms light and airy, and to expose the view of the patio garden through the open living area. Both bathroom doorways were closed off to make space for a walk-in pantry, which was created using a dry-wall construction, and painted in a soft shade of white. We installed lots of open shelves for storage and display, as well as two workbenches that were turned into mobile butcher's blocks for easy food preparation. We chose low-voltage lights on a cable to add a modern touch. The main wall in the kitchen was painted with damp-proof Plascon Double Velvet in Degas (E12-2). For continuity and a good balance of colour and light, the remaining walls were painted in a soft white. We replaced the old sink with a stainless-steel sink that is set in a wooden unit, and we fitted new taps. In addition, we installed a stainless-steel prep bowl.

update your kitchen

The modern kitchen is a wonder to behold and far removed, in both function and style, from the kitchens of old. In many a household the kitchen has become a multi-functional room, where much time is spent. It has become the centre of the home, and the place where everything comes together.

With hectic lifestyles and schedules that clash, the kitchen has become the one room where we can quickly stop to have a chat, or leave a message informing household members of our whereabouts. It's where we (usually) find missing keys, can make shopping lists, and leave hurried notes.

The kitchen is often the only place to find a chair, sit down, and have a nice relaxing cup of tea or to make a phone call. So it is well worth the effort to try and make the kitchen perfect and to ensure that it suits the lifestyle and needs of every member of your household.

When choosing your kitchen style, bear in mind that the finer details, such as work surfaces, paint colours, units, handles, splashbacks and flooring, often make the most impact. Many of which can be changed or updated as your style or your needs change. So don't feel constrained if you can't afford a complete renovation.

Kitchen styles

Eclectic

Highly original and certainly not conventional, this style requires that you have a keen eye for design and perhaps a good sense of humour. Basically, it's a hotchpotch combination of different elements that somehow all work well together in the end.

Open-plan

The open-plan kitchen is perfect for those who like to cook and entertain simultaneously. Knock down the wall between the kitchen and the living room and decorate both in a complementary fashion. Create one spacious room, with two separate functional areas.

Minimalist

Sleek and smooth, you need a fair amount of discipline in order to carry off this look successfully. Space, light and an absence of detail are key elements. Storage is discreet and all the fittings, fixtures and appliances are streamlined.

Retro

Furniture with an industrial edge, wood laminates and linear shapes of mid-20th century design are key elements to this cool look. Stainless steel is the main feature, while marble, terrazzo, glass mosaics and timber veneers complete the picture.

Modern-traditional

Marry modern conveniences with traditional architecture. Stark white walls and wood, and tiles laid in a brickwork pattern are offset by vibrant accessories and designer furniture. Linoleum flooring looks fresh and modern in a bright colour and pattern, while drawer handles and panelled doors echo the style of the kitchens of old.

Farmhouse

This look is all about attention to detail and quality craftmanship. Must-have elements include rustic flooring, limed, panelled or moulded cupboard doors, open shelves, wicker baskets, a laboratory sink, and antique taps.

Classic

This style is a favourite with many families. The surface is low-maintenance and also child-proof. The style is reinforced with glass-fronted cupboards that have traditional push-back catches – ideal for those who collect china and would like to put these items on display.

Left An open-plan kitchen is perfect for entertaining. The huge blackboard adds a bit of whimsy, and useful for shopping lists, lunch menus or notes.
Opposite The focus of this farmhouse kitchen is a solid wood butcher's block.

Kitchen lay-out

Lay-out rather than size determines how well a kitchen functions. Understanding the basics of kitchen lay-out will be invaluable in planning major renovations and may provide ideas for making small but useful improvements in an existing kitchen.

Consider the following essential functions:

◄ Food preparation and cooking
◄ Washing up
◄ Storage
◄ Eating and entertaining

Planning the perfect lay-out

Draw a scale plan of your kitchen. Mark existing plumbing points, windows and doors, as these will influence the positioning of the other elements. Reduce the dimensions of all the elements you want in your kitchen; draw these on extra paper and cut them out. This will allow you to arrange and re-arrange the lay-out until you are satisfied that you have the best possible combination.

Position the essentials

The distance between the stove, sink and fridge should be short, free of obstructions, and allow for an easy flow between food preparation, cooking and washing up. Existing plumbing and wiring will influence the positioning of the stove and sink. Moving pipes and fixtures can be costly, so make sure the new lay-out will be an improvement before committing to it. Once you have found the best positions for the stove, sink and fridge, you can plan and position work surfaces, storage and other major appliances.

Food preparation

Allow at least one metre of work surface for food preparation, more if space allows, and easy access to the fridge. The arrangement of the cooking area will depend on the size of your household and your lifestyle. Singles can get by with only a hob and microwave; families and those who like to entertain will need a hob and oven or a heavy-duty range. If you enjoy baking, consider installing an eye-level oven. Should you install a gas hob, don't forget to provide space for the gas cylinder. A heat-resistant work surface next to the hob is a must. Use it as landing space for hot pots and pans.

Washing up

The sink is usually placed along an outer wall near water supply and drainage. It makes sense to position the dishwasher nearby. Install power and water supply for a dishwasher, even if you don't have one at the moment – it will save a lot of hassle if you want to get one later, and may be of value for the next owner.

Install a double sink if possible – even if you have a dishwasher you will still need a deep sink for washing pots and large platters. If you have a separate scullery, you will need a small rinsing sink or prep bowl in your food preparation area. Allow enough room to work on the side of the sink, as well as to stack dirty dishes. If space is limited, consider a wall-mounted drying-rack, but keep in mind that the drip area below the rack must be waterproof and well sealed around the edges.

Storage

Plan cupboard space to suit the items they are to store – large, wide shelves for pots and pans and narrow-spaced shelves for bottles and packets. Position tall units, such as grocery cupboards so that they do not interrupt the work surface.

Open shelves are great for displaying items such as glasses and plates, but this leaves them exposed to dust and grease. Compromise by using glass-fronted cupboards instead. Be clever with your use of space, and fit as much storage units as possible. A clutter-free kitchen looks larger and cleaner!

Appliances

Even though small appliances are mobile, you still need to take them into account when planning your kitchen. The heat and steam from a kettle or toaster can damage the cupboards. Badly positioned appliances will take up valuable workspace. Cluster small appliances where they do not interrupt the main work surface, and store those that you do not use very often.

Save space by placing the microwave on an eye-level shelf, and the washing machine under a counter. Also make sure that you fit enough power points for all your appliances.

Eating and entertaining

In an open-plan kitchen with a counter, consider making the counter high enough to hide dirty dishes from those seated in the living area. Place the breakfast counter or dining table outside of the main flow of kitchen activity.

Our house: THE KITCHEN

before

The dark, dull and dated kitchen was blocked between four walls, with two doors leading to both bathrooms. We kicked off our Dream House project by knocking out internal walls to make the rooms more spacious. If it sounds like a big job – it was! And even though there are separate areas, the house has a real feeling of spaciousness and balance.

after

We did away with one wall, which means the new light and airy kitchen opens straight into the living area with a view onto the patio garden. We ripped out the old kitchen units and fitted open-shelf working units, which we painted in a soft shade of white to complement the style of the rest of the house. We opted for a white colour scheme for easy mix and match options. We kept the terracotta floor tiles, because they are still in good condition and blend beautifully with the wooden floors of the open-plan living area. We then closed off the entrance to both bathrooms and made space for a much-needed pantry, with lots of open shelves for storage. For this we used a dry-wall installation. The new open-plan lay-out is much more sociable and inviting.

Work surfaces

Choosing the right surface

Work surfaces should be functional and easy to clean. Here are a few options to consider.

Granite

Granite worktops are costly, but also practically impossible to damage, and very easy to clean. A granite work surface is the ideal choice for the sleek modern kitchen. It is non-porous and impervious to food acid, heat and stains. As granite is heavy, you will have to reinforce your base cupboards. Dark granite worktops work well with rich wood units. FYI: the word granite comes from the Latin *granum*, meaning grain, as it is made up of the crystals grains of minerals, such as quartz.

Concrete

Concrete is a very popular choice. It can be cast in virtually any shape and has a robust and seamless surface. It is mixed with additives that make it less susceptible to chipping, then sealed and finally polished. Concrete work tops that have not been sealed properly will stain very easily.

Wood

Wood is full of character and adds warmth and colour to almost any kitchen style. Direct heat and knife cuts will damage the surface. Seal the worktop with polyurethane sealer, water-repellent oil, or varnish. Mix metallic-fronted appliances with painted wooden units to help bounce light around the room. Wood can change colour over time, particularly if the room receives a lot of sun. Clean wooden worktops with water (rather than household cleaners) and dry off. Oiling also helps to clean wood worktops.

Tiles

Tile worktops have a rustic feel, are hard-wearing, waterproof, heat and stain resistant, and easy to clean. Ceramic tiles come in a variety of colours and patterns. They are usually set into cement or stuck straight onto a baseboard and grouted in. Opt for a stainproof grout in a colour that blends well with the tiles. Clean with a damp cloth and a mild detergent. Bear in mind that although tiles are hard, they may eventually crack or chip due to a lot of wear and tear.

Laminate

Laminated worktops are affordable and available in a variety of colours. They are economical, waterproof (if the edges are sealed properly), easy to clean and heat resistant. The only disadvantage is that knife cuts cause damage and the surface does deteriorate over time.

Melamine

A melamine work surface is an inexpensive alternative to real wood. Like laminated worktops, it is economical and waterproof, provided the edges are sealed properly.

Stainless steel

This is the near-perfect worktop material and the choice of chefs everywhere. It is strong, heat-proof and low-maintenance. The only disadvantage is that it scratches easily and shows finger and watermarks.

To offset a cold stainless-steel look, choose base units with a wood finish. For a modern splashback, cover kitchen walls with stainless-steel panels.

Marble and limestone

Marble is heat-proof and available in a range of colours. It is cold and hard and not as durable as granite. Both marble and limestone are porous and will stain if not properly treated with a penetrating sealer.

tip

If you are tall and find it uncomfortable to work on standard height work surfaces (the standard height is 900 mm, with a width of 600 mm) opt for a variety of worktop heights. This way there will be at least one area that is practical for each member of the household. Tall units are usually 2 000 mm high and a wall-mounted unit is about half the depth of a base unit.

Appliances such as stoves, fridges and dishwashers are generally 600 mm wide. If you like the look of an unfitted kitchen, one option is to avoid having standard units all round the room. Supplement your main working areas with extra pieces of furniture, which can be any shape or size.

Choose a honed finish, which is much like an eggshell finish, that will prevent scratches from showing as much as they would on a polished marble surface. Wipe up spills immediately and avoid contact with acids – including citrus juices, wine, cola cooldrinks and curry.

Solid surfaces
These surfaces are extremely costly. They include synthetic solid colour resin materials and composites, which combine resin with chips of stone, glass or mirror. They are durable, hard-wearing and seamless. They can be formed in any shape but are difficult to install without professional help.

What to consider when choosing and replacing work surfaces
When you revamp your kitchen cupboard units, you may want to replace your countertop or work surface as well. This will generally be cheaper than trying to revamp the existing countertop. The hardware store will use the old countertop as a template for the new one. Choose from the following afford-able materials: laminate, stainless steel, slate or tiles. Laminate is

Above left to right Work surfaces, such as wood and granite, are both functional and decorative. They are key elements to creating the overall look of the kitchen.

popular but you'll need to protect it from scratches and hot pots. Stainless steel is durable but may dent. The grout lines of a tiled counter top dirty easily and need frequent cleaning. For this reason, epoxy grout is recommended.

tips
◄ Hang up utensils to keep worktops clutter free, or arrange them in a heavy, wide-neck jar.
◄ A magnetic knife rail will keep knives close at hand, without taking up valuable worktop space.
◄ You could replace only the worktops of existing units. Wood laminate and stainless steel are the best options, as they can be made to order.
◄ Extend your kitchen's worksurface with a butcher's block or small workbench.

Lighting

Because of the amount of time spent in a kitchen, and the demands of the activities that take place there, kitchen lighting should be practical and well planned. The food preparation, cooking and washing-up areas need to be well lit, whether you are working at night or during the day.

Consider the following in your planning:

◀ Where do you need stronger light?
◀ How many fixtures do you need?
◀ Do you want the light source to be above or below?
◀ What can you afford?

Electric light

The most effective kitchen lighting is a combination of general and task lighting. Remember to plan your lighting in such a way that you don't work in your own shadow (i.e. the light source should not be situated behind you).

General lighting

Also known as ambient lighting, it serves as a substitute for daylight and illuminates the whole room. Track lighting, ceiling-mounted spotlights, pendant fixtures, downlighters and fluorescent tubes all provide suitable general light. Bright fluorescent lighting can be harsh and cold; make sure you choose warm-tone tubes.

Task lighting

Task lighting illuminates specific work areas, such as the stove or sink. Directional ceiling spots and track lights can be used as dual purpose general and task lighting, and tend to flatter almost any room. Fluorescent tubes placed below wall-mounted cupboards will provide shadow-free work surface illumination. Conceal the light source with a baffle, as the bright light can be distracting and irritating.

Accent lighting

If your kitchen is fitted with glass-fronted display cupboards, or if you have open shelves with beautiful crockery, you may consider fitting accent lighting to show these off to maximum effect. Restrict accent lighting to shelves and areas that are clean and worth accentuating.

Natural light

Kitchens, especially in older houses, are often starved of natural light. Natural light will make a room appear larger and cleaner and can transform any dingy-looking kitchen. Make the most of existing light by keeping curtains light and simple. Blinds and opaque window film are effective options.

If you're remodelling your kitchen, consider enlarging the windows, or fitting a skylight. Or break out a wall between the kitchen and dining room.

The open-plan kitchen

Lighting is an effective way to define separate areas that share the same space, such as a kitchen and dining area. With well-placed lighting, you can turn the kitchen into a dining room at the flick of a switch. Hang a pendant fitting over the table or kitchen counter to define the dining area, and consider fitting a dimmer switch on the kitchen lights so that the surrounding area fades into the background.

If you have a counter between the kitchen and living/dining area, make sure it's high enough to block the view of dirty dishes from anyone seated at the dining table or on the couch.

Light fittings for the kitchen

The kitchen tends to be a hot and steamy place, so choose light fittings accordingly. Don't select elaborate fittings unless you are prepared to take them down and clean them regularly.

Depending on your kitchen lay-out, the stove might be a difficult area to illuminate. You need shadow-free light in order to see what you are cooking, but avoid a pendant fitting here, as it will only act as a grease trap.

Track lighting is an effective way of combining general, task and accent lighting. See Create the Look on page 68 for instructions on how to install it yourself.

Opposite The accent lighting in this kitchen doubles up as display lighting, showing off the modern clean lines to maximum effect.

Fitted on a cable, these low-voltage track lights add a modern touch, and offer specialised lighting in task areas. The bulbs provide a general white glow and can be used to direct focused light on specific worktops. The tungsten-halogen bulbs provide a crisp and clear light, and they are much brighter than regular bulbs.

create the look

you will need:

✓ 150V transformer
✓ 7 x 12V bulbs
✓ tensioning adjusters:
   one mounting kit with
   turn buckles
✓ wiring
✓ 7 brackets
✓ insulated wire strippers
✓ long-nosed pliers

✓ drill
✓ assorted masonry
   drill-bit set
✓ cross-slot screwdriver
✓ tape measure
✓ pencil
✓ wall plugs
✓ screws
✓ hooks

The transformer unit converts 240V mains electricity into a safer 12V current.
The transformers are also given a watt rating, so a 60W unit can run three 20W lamps.
The open-wire system is completely safe, provided it has been installed properly, because it carries only 12 volts. This means it poses no danger, even if you accidentally touch one of the active terminals. For added peace of mind, you can buy cable that has a protective plastic coating.

how to:

1. Fix the transformer to the wall, above the area for the hooks in step 2. Drill holes and insert a wall plug, then screw in the transformer. Don't plug it in until you have completed all eight steps.

2. Drill holes in the walls at both ends of the room, an equal distance from the ceiling and 6 cm apart, ensuring that the tracks will be parallel. Insert wall plugs and fix hooks.

3. Use pliers to divide the cable in half, creating two light cables.

   Use the brackets to create a loop on one end of each cable. Screw the nut tightly to hold firm.

4. Attach the tension adjusters to these loops and use them to hang the cables on the two hooks on the opposite end of the wall from the transformer.

5. Pull the cables to the hooks opposite and make loops with the brackets, as in step 3. Attach to the hooks.

Note: Leave two long ends to reach the transformer. The tracks shouldn't sag, but you can adjust the tension once the lights are in place.

6. Strip away 10 mm of plastic on the ends of the track, twist the wires together and push it into the holes in the transformer's 12V terminal block. Tighten the screws.

7. Fit the cable connectors to the ends of the metal rods that support the bulbs. Tighten, but don't use too much pressure or you may bend the metal.

8. Fix the rods to the tracks and check that the screws connecting the rods to the cable, pierce the coating and wire. Push in low-voltage bulbs and tighten the small screws on the connectors to hold them in place. Plug into the mains socket.

If you have a problem

If one or two lamps don't work, it's probably a loose connection or a broken bulb. Unplug the transformer and check that all the connections on cables, rods and bulbs are tight. If a bulb blows, replace it immediately or it may damage the fitting. If none of the lamps light up, check the connections at the transformer terminal. Always disconnect from the mains supply when making adjustments.

tips

◄ If your cable is over six metres long, with more than seven bulbs, you will need to set up another circuit with another transformer.

◄ Don't handle tungsten-halogen bulbs with your bare hands. Grease from your skin will mark the bulb and shorten its life. Use a soft cloth, or wear gloves when handling them.

◄ Employ a professional electrician to tackle electrical work that you don't feel confident doing yourself.

Note: Electricity is potentially dangerous. Make sure that you understand how it works before doing any electrical work in your house. Even wiring a plug incorrectly could trip the electrical system in your home. Faulty wiring could very easily cause a fire.

Plumbing and fittings

Leaking taps are a common problem in many kitchens. If you have a wooden or melamine kitchen surface around the sink, a leaking tap could, over time, cause it to swell and even rot. Always keep spare seals and washers on hand and fix the problem the moment you notice it.

How to change a washer

Turn off the main water supply. Turn on the tap to allow all the water to drain. Loosen the tap head and the covers that protect the head of the tap. Use a spanner to unscrew the head. Unscrew the brass nut on the washer plate and replace it with a new one. Make sure the smooth side of the washer is on top. Tighten the brass retaining nut. Screw the head back and then tighten it. Make sure the tap is open when doing this. Close the tap before turning the water supply back on. Follow the same procedure for mixer taps.

tip

To make drainage and general maintenance easier, water pipes should be fixed to exterior walls.

Washing up area

When planning your new kitchen, you need to consider which materials will work best for you, as well as which designs.

Sinks

A new sink can instantly update your kitchen. Stainless-steel sinks come in standard sizes, and range from same-size double basins, to one large and one smaller bowl, or a single basin, all usually with an attached drainage area. While porcelain sinks can be quite costly, they are very attractive and look good in almost any kitchen, particularly those with wood finishes. Synthetic solid surface material sinks have to be custom installed, making them very expensive. The result, however, is seamless, smooth and very sleek.

The twin-basin sinks are the most practical. particularly if you have a large family, or if you enjoy entertaining. Compact, single-basin sinks are far better suited to smaller kitchens. The best option is a deep, rectangular shape, as round or oval basins tend to make the task of cleaning large pots and pans extremely difficult.

A boxy laboratory sink is a traditional design that works well. It is wide and deep, and because it is fitted without a frame, there is only a short distance to reach over into the sink.

A prep bowl is a great addition to your kitchen, if space allows. This nifty little stainless-steel bowl allows for a separate sink in which to wash vegetables.

Splashbacks

Splashbacks made from mosaic tiles, glass or fashionable stainless steel are functional and stylish alternatives to ordinary tiles.

Note: When opting for a splashback, make sure you have enough bare wall space to fit a fold-down, wall-mounted drying rack, a small cabinet or a peg rail.

Taps

A wide variety of taps are available, from single-lever taps to mixers or separate pillar taps. To avoid those dreadful drips, choose taps that are fitted with ceramic discs. Look for taps with a hard, smooth finish. Chrome-coated brass taps remain shiny for years. Nickel-plated taps cost more, while heavy-duty plastic taps are a much cheaper alternative.

Electrical plug points

When planning your new kitchen, make sure you provide enough plug points for all your fixed and mobile appliances. It's better to plan properly before you start tiling and painting.

If you have an old house with only one plug point per room, work out where you would like to fit more points, and don't forget to plan for future appliances such as a dishwasher or tumble dryer. Use a qualified electrician to do the job.

tip

Never underestimate the importance of safety in your home, especially where electricity is concerned. Always ensure that large appliances such as refrigerators, washing machines and tumble dryers have their own plug points.

Water and electricity savers

◄ Don't leave appliances plugged into sockets when they're not in use.

◄ Whenever possible, use the microwave oven and electric frying pan rather than the stove, which uses far more electricity.

◄ When using the kettle, boil only as much water as is needed. The more water you use, the longer it takes to boil, and the more it costs.

◄ Install a time switch on the distribution board to regulate the geyser, switching it on and off at specified times when hot water is not required.

◄ Make sure that hot water taps don't leak. This causes the geyser to heat up constantly, and wastes electricity, as well as water.

◄ Switch lights off when not in use. Opt for low-wattage light bulbs, where possible.

◄ Switch the geyser off at the mains whenever you go away for the weekend or on holiday.

◄ Defrost your fridge regularly and always make sure the doors seal properly.

Far left A prep bowl, used to rinsing vegetables, salad and fruit, is an advantage in any kitchen.

Above A deep laboratory sink is great for cleaning pots and pans, and adds a touch of nostalgia to the overall look.

Storage

You can never have enough storage space – especially in the kitchen. Here are some ideas on how to increase and save space in your kitchen.

Basic storage solutions

◄ Keep lids of pots close at hand in simple wooden racks.

◄ Protect wine glasses. Suspend them from an under-the-cabinet rack.

◄ Store the contents of a messy cupboard on stepped shelves so you can easily see items at the back.

◄ Use wine corks to create a message board. Using a glue gun and plywood, glue the corks lengthwise to the wood; start in a corner and position two corks vertically; then two horizontally. Continue the pattern until the plywood is covered. Frame the board with strips or molding.

◄ Mix under-bench and floor-to-ceiling units, as well as open and closed storage.

◄ Group taller kitchen cupboard units together to create the illusion of more space.

◄ Open shelves are versatile and cost-effective.

◄ Fit a hanging rail below units so you can keep equipment close at hand.

◄ In a large, square kitchen, position the table in the centre and line the walls with appliances and units for maximum storage space.

◄ A slim-line, pull-out unit next to the cooktop is ideal for storing oils, sauces and seasoning.

◄ Keep kitchen utensils or fruit in a wire basket.

◄ Line up matching storage jars for maximum effect.

◄ Display dry foods in decorative jars on shelves.

◄ A handy spice rack is a neat worktop accessory.

◄ For interest, combine open shelves with solid-fronted units.

Food storage

If space allows, a separate pantry is an enormous space-saver in the kitchen. Pantries should be cool, dark and well-ventilated, easy to access, with plenty of shelving.

Above The kitchen's focal wall, with wooden shelving, makes the most of the room's height. Cost-effective features, such as wooden worktops, and workbenches with open storage, have a strong visual impact.

Opposite left and right Open-faced or hanging storage will keep essentials in sight, but out of the way.

Mobile storage

Baskets are a plus in any room in the house. Store kitchen equipment (from utensils to dishcloths) in different-sized baskets. If you can't find a basket shape, size or colour that you like, visit your local Society for the Blind outlet – they will make you a basket to suit your specific needs.

Another great option – especially in small kitchens, is to invest in a central unit or butcher's block on lockable casters that can be wheeled out of the way, freeing up valuable floor space. You can give new life to a workbench (available at any hardware store), by adding casters to the base and converting it into a mobile work island. Cover the top with a heat-resistant surface and hang utensils from a steel rack on opposite sides.

Laundry storage

A seperate laundry is a dream come true for most of us. Due to a lack of space, more and more people are forced to house their laundry in a cupboard within the kitchen or bathroom. If this is the case in your house, here are some valuable tips.

◀ Make sure the space is well ventilated, with plenty of natural light and a good airflow to minimise dampness and mildew.
◀ Install an extractor fan, and use a wall paint with an anti-mould agent.
◀ Make sure that the moist air from the tumble dryer is vented outdoors.
◀ Open shelving is ideal for storing cleaning equipment.
◀ Minimise clutter with a pull-out (or ceiling hung) drying rail, a flip-down ironing board, and lots of laundry baskets for all your washing needs.

◀ If your washing machine and tumble dryer are located in the kitchen, place them behind cupboard doors. It looks neater and will cut down on some of the noise.
◀ Save space – stack the washing machine and tumble dryer.
◀ Invest in concertina doors to separate the laundry space from the rest of the kitchen.

tip

◀ For an unusual wine rack, use lengths of ordinary white, plastic piping, shorten it and stack it against the wall in an alcove or inside a cupboard.

makeover tips for old kitchen units

◀ Update old wooden or melamine units with modern bar handles and chrome accessories.
◀ Simple brushed-chrome knobs add a neat, modern touch to kitchen drawers.
◀ Change the insets of your kitchen cupboards for a more contemporary look. Try punched hardboard and paint it white. The holes in the hardboard provide good ventilation and prevent the inside of the cupboards from becoming musty.

Flooring

Ideal flooring for kitchens

The kitchen floor needs to be impermeable, so unsealed soft wood really is not an option. There are a number of hard-wearing, slip-, water- and stain-resistant options from which to choose. Bear in mind that hard flooring such as stone, concrete and terracotta can be most unforgiving when you're standing for a long time. They aslo accentuate noise.

Stone

A stone floor works well in areas that extend from indoors to out, but it is very costly. Stone tiles are less expensive and not as heavy as stone slabs. Bear in mind that a stone floor will be rather chilly during winter.

Concrete

Concrete is durable, affordable, and heat and scratch resistant. To make it more chic, mix coloured oxides into the cement before it is poured. When it is cured, seal the surface with several coats of acrylic or epoxy resin so it doesn't soak up spills.

Tiles

Durable and easy to clean, tiles are a popular choice for the kitchen. Choose tiles that are non-slip, and a practical colour. Large tiles, laid in diagonal lines, will make the floor surface appear less 'square'.

Cork

Cork tiles are soft and warm. The thicker the tile you use, the more resilient your floor will be. Lay cork tiles on a flat surface and seal with four coats of polyurethane or polymer sealant to protect it.

Vinyl

Vinyl is waterproof, oil-proof and easy to clean. It is sold as tiles or sheets and contains PVC (polyvinyl chloride), which gives it flexibility. Vinyl wears best when laid over a flat floor, but can be laid over existing flooring. The downside is that it doesn't age well, and scratches fairly easily.

Rubber

Rubber flooring is warm and also very hard-wearing. Unfortunately, if it is smooth, rubber can get very slippery when wet. In which case you should rather opt for a studded pattern.

If left unpolished and matt, rubber will mark very easily. You will do well to protect it with a layer of water-soluble wax emulsion polish.

Linoleum

Linoleum is eco-friendly and durable. It is made of linseed oil, ground cork, wood, flour and resin, which is baked and pressed onto a jute or hessian backing. You can buy it in the form of sheeting, or as tiles. Lay it on a flat timber or fibreboard floor.

tips

‹ Combine two types of flooring for an interesting design, but lay the more durable surface below the sink.
‹ Pour concrete over ugly tiled floors or remove the tiles and screed the floor (see flooring page 32).
‹ Seal wooden floorboards in the kitchen, but keep in mind that sealants wear off and must be reapplied. You can also paint or whitewash floorboards.

how to replace a broken tile

‹ Cut out the grout around the edges of the damaged tile with a grout saw, or scrape it free with the tip of an old screwdriver. Work slowly to avoid chipping the edges of the surrounding tiles.
‹ Wear safety goggles for this step. Use a sharp, cold chisel and a ball-peen hammer to crack the tile in an X-pattern. Tap lightly to avoid damaging the other tiles. Pry out the pieces and chip out the old adhesive.
‹ Spread 3 mm of tile adhesive on the back of the replacement tile, press in place, and use tape or spacers to hold it. Scrape excess adhesive from the gaps and wipe clean. Let the adhesive cure.
‹ Press grout into the joins and smooth it. Wipe off the excess grout with a damp sponge. Use a dry cloth to polish off any haze that forms on the tile surface.

Our house: THE LAUNDRY

before

The dilapidated outside room, just off the kitchen, housed a separate toilet and cistern with chain, some ugly shelving, with a washbasin behind the door. It was in disrepair and in desperate need of renovating. Without breaking the bank, we transformed this 2 m x 2 m room into an outside washing room that could easily accommodate a washing machine and tumble dryer.

after

We removed the toilet, cistern, old ceilings and rotten shelving. We closed all the holes and re-plastered the walls. We used skimmed Rhinoboard for the new ceiling. We then built a small wall with brick and plaster to make space for a washing machine and tumble dryer. We installed new water pipes and electrical plugs for the washing machine. In keeping with the rest of the house, we painted the room in a soft white using the Plascon Velvaglo range, which is damp-proof. To the left of the room, on top of the washing machine and tumble dryer, we installed shelving to store baskets, laundry and washing products. We also removed the glass outside door and replaced it with a solid wooden door for easy lock-up purposes. For use on rainy days, we installed a pull-out washing line.

Finishing touches

Getting the look, country style

With a few good pieces of kitchen furniture and accessories (whether they're inherited or bought), the country look is easily achieved. Second-hand furniture shops and auction houses are good sources for interesting finds. Add your individual stamp in the way you arrange the objects.

◀ Choose natural, earthy colours (such as straw, buttermilk, rust, teal and muted blues) for walls and furniture.

◀ A large, rustic wooden table with a selection of comfortable chairs or benches is a must. Paint or distress a few chairs (or the table) to add colour and brighten the room.

◀ Invest in white or cream crockery and mix and match with old pieces of crockery, silver, pewter and enamelware to create interesting table settings.

◀ Shop around second-hand stores for old linen napkins, preferably white or cream. Stitch a few together to make a matching tablecloth or runner, or use them to make bistro-style curtains by clipping them onto a thin rod.

◀ Clear clutter and create clever storage, using wicker baskets, wooden crates and even old milk pails, to keep things tidy.

◀ Display items for everyday use in interesting ways – the secret is to group items of a similar height together – and have open shelving for easy access.

◀ Invest in slate, granite or durable wooden work surfaces, and install old-fashioned basins and copper fittings. Practical flooring options include wood, slate and clay tiles or painted cement.

◀ Start a kitchen garden and decorate it with old-fashioned rusted implements.

Window dressing/blinds

The trend towards fuss-free window treatments and curtain clips means it is easy to dress windows using the fabric of your choice.

Fresh paint

For an uncluttered feel, paint walls and ceilings white and select flat-fronted units. Off-white walls increase the sense of space. Play with darker and lighter tones of a single colour to add

definition between walls. Alternatively, make a feature of one of the walls. This works well in a space that does not have a focal point. Use the same colour, but change the finish (matt, high-gloss, or pearlised).

tips

◀ Sand doors lightly and apply a multi-surface primer before you paint. Your local hardware store will be able to advise you on what to use.

◀ Avoid painting a kitchen work surface as the paint may be damaged by hot pots and cutting utensils.

Other inexpensive options:

◀ Replace the doorknobs with slimline chrome handles.

◀ Paint your walls in different shades of the same colour for added interest.

◀ Use free-standing units such as a trolley or dresser to show off your crockery collection, if you have space.

◀ Source interesting pieces of furniture for your kitchen, or buy new chairs for your table to create a modern feel.

◀ Give the windows a splash of colour with an attractive blind or curtains.

◀ Complete the look with modern accessories, such as a new kettle, toaster, wall clock, scale and collander.

quick-'n-easy kitchen update

If you're tired of your old melamine kitchen cupboards, but can't afford to replace them, why not paint the cupboards in your favourite colour scheme?

you will need:

✓ Plascon melamine primer
✓ Plascon Velvaglo Satin
✓ Polycell filler
✓ Polycell sugar soap solution
✓ Sandpaper
✓ Paintbrush
✓ Roller and tray

how to:

1. Make sure that surfaces are clean and dry before painting. Remove door handles. Sand surface lightly. Fill all defects with appropriate Polycell filler.
2. Remove mould with household bleach and rinse with water. Remove grease or oil with a sugar soap solution, particularly around the stove and in food preparation areas. Allow to dry.
3. Stir the melamine primer and apply a thin coat using a brush or roller. Allow to dry for 24 hours.
4. Paint cupboards with a coat of Velvaglo Satin, using a brush or roller. Allow to dry for 24 hours.

Opposite and top left The secret to effectively displaying functional items, such as utensils and glasses, is to create unity by repeating colour or form.

inviting living areas

The modern living area has become just as multi-functional as the modern kitchen. It's a place to relax and unwind with a good book, or a bottle of fine wine and close friends, watching television or listening to a favourite CD. Combining all these functions and allowing you to display your individual style, the modern living room has to be practical, and aesthetically pleasing.

Creating an inviting living area, involves a multitude of decisions about colour and light, furniture, and decorative features – all influenced by space, as well as your budget. Always start by considering your family's needs, and then move on to basics such as lighting, mouldings and fitted fixtures. These are the fixed elements that will remain part of the house and could add value, should you decide to sell.

Your home is an extension of your personality and style, and decorating it is a wonderful opportunity to interpret basic decorating principles in your own unique way. It's a fun activity, and you can do it over and over again, as many times as your taste and style will change – as long as you remain practical. A pure-white lounge suite may look quite eye-catching in a magazine, but it's certainly not suitable for a family room filled with slobbering dogs and children with dirty hands and feet.

Lighting

Light, whether it be natural or artificial, is one of the most powerful decorating tools. It can influence the perceived dimensions of a room, it can enhance or disguise certain features, and it plays an important part in setting the general ambience within a room.

Types of lighting

Ambient lighting is a general daylight substitute that illuminates the entire room. To cast a flat and even glow across a room, and to provide an overall effect that is soft and diffuses the light in the room, use any combination of ceiling-fixed, wall-mounted or floor-standing lamps, wall sconces or recessed ceiling fixtures. Dimmer switches can be used with ambient lighting to soften the light and to create more atmosphere.

Task lighting is used to illuminate a specific area, such as a reading corner or dining-room table. It is bright and functional, and is attained through using spotlights, adjustable table and floor lamps, bedside lamps and undercounter lighting. Lights that are adjustable serve this function best.

Accent lighting is used to highlight objects such as sculptures, paintings and plants, and can be used to great dramatic effect. Wall-mounted lights and floor lights can be used for this purpose. They typically use halogen bulbs because of the intensity of light they produce. Traditional picture lights are always a safe bet as they eliminate the glare and shadows caused by the frames. When using accent lighting, bear in mind that the bulbs should be no more than three times as bright as the ambient lighting, and no fixtures should block your line of sight, or cause a glare.

Where to start

Planning the lighting for your home should be one of the first steps in the makeover process. Start by drawing a floor plan that includes the windows, doors, sliding doors and furniture placements, the location of electrical points and switches and any other permanent features such as a fireplace. Also make a note of the objects in the room that you would like to emphasise, and where you will be performing tasks that require special lighting. Also consider whether you want the light source to be above or below. Now you should consider the practical implications. Does your new plan fit in with existing light and power points? Will your budget cover the cost of the electrician and the new fixtures? Revise your plan, if necessary, so that you spend your money on only a few, really well-placed fixtures.

Choosing light fixtures

Finding the right fixtures isn't always easy. Cost and size vary, so it's important to list beforehand what you need and what will complement the style of décor best.

You will have to decide whether you want the light fixture to be part of the décor, or whether you would like it to be unobtrusive or recessed. In addition to the style of the fixture, you need to consider what it looks like when switched on, and whether it casts the right type of light.

Large, dramatic fixtures, such as chandeliers, are back in vogue, and there are various styles, shapes and colours from which to choose. Select a large striking example to add drama, or a smaller, more delicate one for a softer feel. Suspend fixtures where light is needed and not simply in the centre of the room. It is often thought that only small fixtures should be used in smaller rooms, but a large, striking fixture could be successfully used as a focal point in a room – drawing attention and setting the trend for the rest of the decorative elements.

Lamps

Lamps are an easy and affordable way to create instant atmosphere and can also be used for accent and task lighting. They are generally easily matched to any decorating style and can add to the overall charm of a room. Always choose bulbs with a low wattage to provide soft light and to prevent covers from being scorched. Keep in mind that coloured translucent lampshades will change the colour of the light. Lamps with long bases and small covers can effectively be used to provide light for reading – choose daylight bulbs, and covers with white insides for crisp light that won't strain the eyes. Opt for a tall standing lamp to cast a soft pool of light over a chair that's used to recline or read in at night.

Light and colour

Different types of lighting provide different colours of light. Often a certain colour scheme – or even an entire room – will appear dull at night, whereas in daytime it appears fresh and appealing. By using the right amount and quality of lighting, colours will be rendered much more accurately, creating the preferred ambience.

If you don't want the colour of a wall to dominate the room, don't use wall lights. This will turn the wall into a huge reflector, only intensifying the colour. Rather paint the ceiling in a neutral shade and hang a fitting from the ceiling to provide colourless, but ambient, light. Keep in mind that translucent coloured lampshades will change the colour of the light.

Fit the right bulbs

Ordinary light bulbs provide yellowish light and complement warmer colours, such as yellow, red and orange. These are best used at low levels of illumination and are perfect for creating ambience at night. Daylight bulbs provide a bluish light and complement the cooler colours, such as blue and green. They are best used at high levels of illumination. Halogen light bulbs provide a clear, crisp light, ideal for showing off vibrant colours, and perfect if you prefer a brightly lit room.

Using coloured light bulbs in a contrasting colour to that of your colour scheme can muddy the colours, and is best avoided, especially in the bedroom.

Natural light

Don't forget about natural light when considering lighting options for your home – a room bathed in natural light always looks warm and appealing.

Windows

Always try to make the most of available natural light. Keep windows free of elaborate window-dressings and opt for simple curtains or blinds instead. Use thin translucent curtains where you would like a little privacy, or to cut out a very strong glare.

If it's a bathroom window and privacy is your main concern, but you'd still like ample natural light, investigate options such as mirrored, frosted or coloured glass.

Skylights

Skylights are an excellent way of providing natural daylight in a room, particularly in older homes with smaller windows, or in dark and narrow passageways. Conventional skylights may let in too much heat and light, but there are a variety of new designs (such as angular-selective skylights) that can be very effective in letting in indirect light.

Quick lighting makeovers

Use candles and fairy lights to instantly transform a room for special occasions, or to create a festive or intimate atmosphere.

Install track lights for quick and effective accent lighting (see Create the Look on page 68).

Re-cover lampshades in an accent colour that will complement your style, but bear in mind that not all fabrics are suitable for lampshades.

Change the position of a central, hanging light fixture. Extend the cord and loop it through a hook, inserted in the ceiling, over the spot where you would like the fixture to hang (check that the hook can hold the weight of the fixture). Even out shadows created by central fixtures by using lamps or by adding a down light in each corner of the room. Brighten your room by adding a mirror or two. The mirrors will reflect natural light into the room, and make the room appear visually larger by creating depth and dimension.

Fitted finishing touches

Attention to architectural detail can make an incredible difference to the style and individuality of a room or an entire house. Elements such as cornices, picture rails, mouldings, skirting boards and original wooden or parquet floors not only add decorative detail, but also emphasise the style and ambience of the interior.

Mouldings

In even the simplest home, adding small touches, such as cornices and skirting boards, will create a well-finished look.

Cornices create balance

A cornice is the moulded strip where wall and ceiling meet; it can be patterned or plain. Older cornices were made of wood or plaster, but nowadays they are made from light wood and even polystyrene. In most cases, cornices form part of the background and should not be noticed at a first glance, otherwise they will detract from the planned focal points and upset the balance of the room. Cornices with a decorative design should be painted the same colour as the ceiling (which will also make the room look slightly larger), but plain cornices can be painted the same colour as the wall. As a rule, cornices are not painted in a contrasting colour to the walls and ceiling.

Skirting boards

Skirting boards are dual-purpose items that protect the wall, and keep the carpeting in place. You can either finish and protect the timber (usually meranti) with a wood sealer, or paint it to match the wall or the floor covering.

Whether you have fitted carpets, or a tiled or a wooden floor, decide whether to match the skirting to the colour of the floor or the wall, depending on which area you wish to emphasise. If your walls and flooring are a neutral colour, consider painting your skirting boards a shade darker than the flooring.

Skirting boards are very practical, but they will get knocked and chipped over time. Keep them well maintained and regularly apply a new coat of paint or varnish finish. Use a good quality matt enamel paint, or a clear wood preservative for added durability.

Picture and dado rails

Picture rails are often overlooked as decorative elements. They can be painted a contrasting colour to visually break a high wall and are, of course, also useful for hanging pictures. Use transparent fishing line to hang your pictures.

Dado or chair rails are positioned a third of the way up a wall. Like skirting boards, they also have a practical function and are used in dining rooms and hallways to protect the wall from knocks. Often the dado rail and the wall below it are painted in a darker contrasting colour to the rest of the wall. This is a good way to disguise scuffs and marks.

Wallpaper dado rails (a frieze rail)

If you'd rather forgo the 3D effect of a moulded dado rail, compromise with a stylish wallpaper border. Wallpaper is coming back into fashion and there are some lovely paper borders in designs ranging from traditional to modern. There are fun prints for nurseries and children's rooms, and elegant patterns and floral or geometric styles to suit any style and room in your home. When selecting a border print, choose one that contrasts with the current wall colour or wallpaper and then note how it changes the character of the interior.

Use mouldings to create balance on plain surfaces

Another way to define wall areas, interior doors, cupboards and wardrobe doors, is to construct a false panel on the surface. Make squares or rectangles with lengths of plain or decorative wooden moulding or beading (available from your local hardware store). Make sure the proportions are correct in relation to the height and width of the ceiling, wall or door, depending on what you wish to panel.

Emphasise panels with a stencilled or paper border, or by painting the border a different colour to that of the background. Make sure the colour blends well with the colour scheme of the room. Alternatively, you could choose to leave the panels plain and just enjoy their texture and shape. They make ideal 'frames' to highlight works of art, each hung within a panel.

Opposite Always try to decorate your home incorporating original fittings. Don't try to disguise them. Here a picture rail has been given a stunning modern twist.

Restoring wooden finishes

The only way to rejuvenate an old wooden floor (wood strips or parquet blocks) is to sand the surface, removing the top layer to reveal the lovely pale texture of the wood beneath. You can either hire someone to do this for you, or you can hire all the necessary equipment and do it yourself. Floors can be sealed with varnish or treated with various paint effects.

Flooring DIY

You will have to hire a large industrial floor sander, and a hand scraper (or a sanding attachment for an electric drill) to get into corners. Purchase medium and fine-grade sandpaper (available with the sander) and a pack of disposable dust masks.
Before treating the newly sanded floors, it is very important to clean the sanded area thoroughly to remove all dust.

Decorative timber treatments

Aging

To recreate the patina of an old Colonial-style floor, the newness of freshly sanded wood needs to be toned down considerably. For a very light to white finish, use bleach. Ordinary household bleach will do, but the process tends to make the timber alkaline. Rinse off the bleaching agent with a solution of vinegar and water in the ratio 1:7.

Now treat the timber with a wire brush to bring up the grain. A light skim coat of plaster filler should be applied then sanded off, before applying three coats of matt, clear polyurethane varnish.

To introduce a hint of colour, sand the timber thoroughly, with medium grade steel wool or sandpaper. Apply a coat of diluted gloss paint in either white, pale grey or pale blue, which are all ideal 'aging' colours. Mix one part white spirit to two parts paint.

When thoroughly dry, apply a second coat of diluted paint, adding a little more white spirit to achieve a slightly lighter shade. Brush this down the centre of each floorboard for an authentic well-trodden look. Finish with two coats of clear matt polyurethane varnish.

Liming

For this effect, use a whitewash or white oil-based paint, diluted until runny with white spirit or turpentine. Paint along the length of the board, working a metre at a time. Work board by board to prevent lines from forming. Immediately wipe the paint off with a clean rag, pulling strokes along the length of the board and leaving paint in the cracks. You will need a good supply of clean dry cloths for this. Allow to dry.

Staining

Wooden floors can also be stained, and apart from natural timber colours there is a wide variety of brightly coloured stains available. Follow the manufacturer's instructions and work quickly, using a soft cloth to rub the stain into the grain.

Painting

If a wooden floor isn't particularly eye-pleasing, paint it! Make sure that the surface is dry and clean and apply several coats of undercoat to act as a primer. Then apply a topcoat of oil-based gloss, eggshell or special floor paint, depending on the type of finish you prefer. Deck or marine paint can also be used and are most durable, but difficult to apply, and takes a long time to dry. Your choice of colours will also be limited.

Doors and window frames

Exterior doors and window frames are prone to weathering – the wood gets bleached by the sun or darkens with age. Solid wood can be stripped to reveal fresh wood underneath. Seal and protect the newly exposed wood with appropriately coloured outdoor timber preservative sealer. Avoid varnish that might crack in hot and direct sunlight.

Modern interior doors are usually hollow and made of plain chipboard or superwood that has a veneered finish or is simply painted. These rather ordinary doors can be made to look quite special when fitted with false panels (see page 82).

Quick makeover for doors

Replace nondescript handles with eye-catching modern or, if you prefer, antique fittings of brass, ceramic, enamelled metal or anodised steel. If possible, follow through with matching cover plates for light and dimmer switches.

sanding and sealing

Although sanding wooden floors is usually a job for a professional, you can do it yourself – sanding machines can be obtained from tool-hiring companies.

Sanding floors is a messy job, so remove all furniture and shelving from the area, if possible. If the wooden floor is on an upper level, the dust will settle on the floor below, so either remove or cover all furniture in this area. Sanders make a lot of noise so be considerate towards neighbours and only use the sander at a reasonable hour.

Avoid spilling anything on a newly sanded floor (before it is sealed).The timber will prevent stain or could swell.

Remove all traces of wood dust with a vacuum cleaner, before applying varnish or sealer. Apply the first coat with a lint-free cloth or sponge or a paint roller, to ensure it sinks into the raw wood. Allow it to dry thoroughly between each application. Subsequent coats can be applied with a brush.

Two coats of sealer should be sufficient in light-traffic areas where rugs will be used. In high-traffic areas, such as kitchens and passages, apply at least three coats.

Right A gloss finish was used to accentuate the grain of the wood floor.

Putting it together

The interior of your home and the way in which everything is put together, should be an expression of your own personal style and of the way you and your family live.

Start by working through Planning on page 16 before putting it all together. Don't feel constrained by a limited budget or lack of decorating experience – follow the basic guidelines and let your imagination lead you the rest of the way.

Aspects such as colour, lighting, furniture and decoration all contribute to the overall atmosphere and style of the room, so it's important that all of these elements work together to create the look you want. The trick is to always work with the end result in mind, and to make sure decorative elements complement each other and create unity in the room.

Don't be tempted by impulse buys that look great in retail displays. You may very well find that the item doesn't contribute much to your existing décor. If you know what you want when you set out, you are much more likely to spend your money on items that will truly contribute to your overall look.

Below Create unity in a room by ensuring that decorative elements complement each other.

Style tips

When it comes to style, it is not about what you buy, but about how you treat each individual piece, and how you put it all together. Furniture and decorative elements will only get you so far – the rest is presentation.

Theme supreme Theming a room might give you some direction in terms of your décor. As long as you don't go overboard. Subtly reflect your theme with colour and decorative elements. Make sure it's easy to create and live with.

Repeat treat A row of identical objects is perfect for creating a dramatic impact. Anything from vases to red apples will look stunning on display. Repeating a particular colour, shape or pattern is just as effective.

Perfect duos If you're not sure which paint to use, choose a single background colour and a complementary accent colour. Look around you for natural combinations, then try them out – be as dramatic or subtle as you like.

Fashionista Create up-to-the-minute looks by covering your cushions with trendy fabric in the latest colours and textures. Use fashionable trimmings such as buttons, pockets, tassels, ribbons and flowers on pillowcases or lampshades. If you do it cleverly, you can change the look of a room with every season (see page 88).

Bold is beautiful All you need to make your home unique is a little imagination. Second-hand stores, office or catering suppliers and even builders' merchants all make great hunting grounds for unusual objects. Always buy objects that *you* like and your home will always have a personalised feel.

Small, medium and large Decorating with a sense of scale can transform an interior. It allows you to play visual tricks with proportion and to give even the smallest displays some drama. Group objects and furnishings by size, rather than by colour or shape, or experiment with using one big object in a room to create some drama.

Wall it all Use your walls! Instead of just displaying pictures, try putting up a few mini shelves for showing off your favourite pieces. You can also use a few hooks to hanging anything from bags to keys, or use your walls to display collections of items such as flat baskets or wall clocks.

Beauty and balance As our notion of beauty is strongly linked to symmetry, anything visually balanced is easy on the eye. Try mirror-image displays, such as tall shelves on either side of a door or fireplace.

Less is more Be ruthless! Completely rid your home of clutter and any objects or items that you don't use and don't really need. Free up some of that valuable space and give your home some room to breathe.

Experiment Don't be rigid. This is your home after all. And although there are rules in terms of style and design principles, the rest is entirely up to you. You may find that your instincts guide you towards interesting combinations, such as a contemporary style with a few vintage pieces. If you do it right, you can create a stylish unity with individual appeal. Set forth, go and create a trend!

Seasonal changes

Rooms that are cool and inviting in summer, often appear chilly and uninviting in winter. This often happens when a room is decorated in either summer or winter. The climate plays a deciding role in the choice of furniture and accessories, which create the look and feel of the room. It is easy to rectify, though, and can be done by changing the accessories to match the season, creating an inviting home all year round.

Where to start?

Have a good look at the room – for example your lounge. What are the predominant colours? Perhaps lots of dark browns, dark wood and calico was used, creating a peaceful, warm effect that is perfect for winter. For summer, however, it would simply be too heavy and drab and in need of some vibrant colours.

Lighten up by packing away clutter, heavy cushions, throws and drapes. Add splashes of crisp, fresh colours (such as turquoise, aqua, lime green, fun pinks and yellows) to introduce the new season and freshen up the room. In winter, drapes and throws and cushions can come out again, providing warmth and places to snuggle. Winter colours are heavier, deeper and more intense – deep, rich reds, burnt oranges, moody purples and rich browns.

Colour

Colour can visually change the way we perceive most things and it is perfect for changing the look of a room without doing too much. For summer, choose a few or even just a single bright, breezy colour to complement or harmonise with an existing

colour scheme. It could be a colour that is already there and is simply a minor feature, or it could be a contrasting colour to add some zing. Use this colour in accessories, such as cushion covers or beading on covers, lampshades, snack bowls, candles and more, and splash it around the room for effect. If the room is decorated in winter colours, brighten it by adding cream and perhaps touches of turquoise, or use fresh green foliage to soften a dark, heavy feel.

For winter, do the exact opposite by adding winter colours to a more summery room to warm it up.

Textures
Winter is the time for comforting textures such as wool, mohair and thick, crocheted throws, heavier, more textured drapes, and upholstered cushions with interesting textures and a warm, cosy feel. Summer calls for a lighter approach, using sheer fabrics, such as voile and cotton, to allow for air flow and light.

Layering
Layering helps to create a luxurious feel in any room. It is a simple decorating trick that can be put to good use – especially in winter. If a room has a definite summery feel, create warmth with layers by combining throws, cushions and bed covers, all with different winter textures for interest and effect. In summer, pack most of those away and opt for crisp, cool cotton sheets and perhaps a crocheted throw that contrasts with the smooth cotton.

Fragrances
Scent your home in winter with cinnamon, spices and mulled-wine fragrances for a cosy, homely effect, and fresh grassy or floral smells in summer for a crisp, fresh feel. Use scented candles, aromatic oils, linen and room sprays, and soaps.

Move around
An effective way of changing décor to suit the season, is to move the furniture around. You can gain light and heat in winter by moving items to a sunny spot or closer to the fireplace. You can change the appearance of the room altogether.

Opposite and above
A well-planned room can be totally transformed by changing decorative elements, such as cushions and vases.

comfortable bedrooms

A place to sleep, and rest, and dream, the bedroom is where you take a time-out from the daily grind of life, where you catch up with yourself after a long and tiring day. Your bedroom should be a personal haven – filled with whatever you need to feel pampered and spoilt. Invest in this, and make your bedroom the most special space in your home.

Busy and stressful lifestyles influence the way we decorate rooms – especially the bedroom. Far from having just the basics, rooms are being tailor-made to suit our individual needs.

Manufacturers and retailers are creating and producing furniture in every imaginable style, shape, size and colour, and there is an amazing array of soft furnishings and bed linen that is forever changing. All of this providing you with an incredible range of options with which you can create your dream room.

The trend has become to not follow trends, and to simply create a room in which you can actually live. All that remain are the basic guidelines as to how best to achieve a certain look, or create the feel of a certain era. And the simple but important rules of colour. Affecting how you feel, colour plays a very important role in the bedroom. Use bright and cheery colours for an up-beat feel and more subdued colours for a peaceful tranquil atmosphere.

Bedroom basics

Clever use of colour, light, furniture and soft furnishings can transform almost any room, large or small, into a comfortable, restful space. Be practical and match your chosen style to the existing room and furnishings (as well as to your budget). Follow these basic principles to ensure that you achieve the best possible results.

Discover your style

There are an amazing number of different bedroom styles from which you can choose. And if you're like most people, you have a good idea of what it is that you want, you're just not very sure how to achieve it.

Browse through magazines and cut out pictures of bedrooms styles that really appeal to you. Take careful note of colours used (main colours, accent and complementary shades) as well as the size, colour and type of furniture. Note also the various decorating accessories and elements used, and the overall style of the rooms – are they formal, traditional, rustic country, modern, romantic or Eastern? Do they seem restful, exciting, fun-filled, traditional or elegant? Or are they perhaps a mix of a few styles?

By doing this, you will learn a lot about which pieces of furniture to combine, which colours will work well together and, above all, which decorative details are needed to finish it off successfully.

Change, take away and add more samples until you are happy with the mix. Once you have found your preferred style, collect paint strips, fabric samples and accessories, and prepare a mood board (see page 22).

Be practical

Always consider how the bedroom will be used. Do you enjoy reading in bed or do you enjoy watching DVDs? These activities will help you determine which furnishings you need to be able to create a bedroom that fulfils all your needs.

If space is limited, reconsider some of the items (or at least their size), until everything you need can fit into the available space. Keep in mind that beds need space around them to allow for traffic, and cupboards to allow for the opening of doors. Too much furniture and too little space will shrink the room's visual size.

Use space efficiently

Increase the perceived size of a room by opting for fewer and larger pieces of furniture. Invest in tall wardrobes (free-standing or built-in) with lots of storage space. Make the most of the available natural light and keep window-dressing light and simple. Look at the way the furniture is arranged and move it around until you find the best way to create more open space.

Remove clutter

Be quite ruthless and remove any pieces of furniture and decorations that you don't really need. Store whatever you don't use or simply throw it away. Go through your wardrobe and clear anything that hasn't been worn for the last two seasons, including accessories such as shoes and bags. Unworn clothing tends to take up loads of valuable space.

Clear the walls

Remove all the drawings and paintings from the walls and arrange fewer and larger groupings on only one wall. Leaving the other walls open will draw attention and add to the illusion of space. Another trick is to hang decorations on the wall furthest from the door, thus drawing the attention through the room – making it appear more spacious.

Adapt and exchange

Have a good look at existing pieces of bedroom furniture. Often certain pieces need simple adjustments to make them more functional and to create extra storage space. For example, add extra shelving to built-in cupboards, or place a low-slung futon on a small deck or castors.

Right Muted neutral tones combined with lots of cool white and textured accessories, create a restful haven.

Redecorate

Changing the colour scheme can do wonders for the appearance of a room. Soft, receding colours from the cooler side of the colour spectrum (e.g. greens, blues, turquoise, etc) painted on walls and present in soft furnishings, will create the illusion of more space. Turn to page 52 for more information about choosing the right shade for the room.

Buying bed linen

◀ Opt for a duvet one size bigger than the bed – it looks more luxurious and provides more duvet under which to snuggle.
◀ Spend more money on quality bed linen and save a little by buying less decorative accessories for your room.
◀ Read labels and, whenever possible, select bedding with a high thread count.

What is thread count?

Thread count refers to the number of threads per 2.5 cm² of fabric, and is used to indicate the quality of the bed linen. Standard thread counts are 180 to 200. Luxury thread counts are 300 and up.

Lighting

Lighting in bedrooms is often overlooked and anything over and above the central ceiling fixture is deemed unnecessary. Proper lighting will not only do wonders for the atmosphere in your bedroom, but soft, dimmed lighting at night will encourage winding down after a long day, while bright light in the early morning will ensure that make-up is done in all the right colours, and that the colour of your socks and shoes match. See page 68 for more general information on lighting.

Practical lighting for bedrooms

◀ When buying a bedside lamp, choose one that beams over only half of the bed. This way it won't disturb the person lying next to you (who's probably trying to sleep). A reading lamp should be tall enough for the light to cast enough illumination on the page you're reading, but the light shouldn't be positioned in such a way that it shines directly into your eyes.
◀ When providing light at dressing tables, choose clear, daylight bulbs to recreate daylight as closely as possible, and position two light sources, one at each side of the table. This will prevent shadows from falling across your face as you apply make-up, etc.
◀ Using coloured light bulbs that contrast with your colour scheme can muddy the hues and is something you should avoid, especially in the bedroom.

Left Be creative when choosing bed linen. Combine various patterns and textures for interest – even if it is all in the same colour scheme. Turquoise and white always create a fresh, crisp feel.
Opposite A few well-chosen decorative elements give this Eastern-inspired bedroom contemporary appeal.

All about cupboards

Cupboards are a basic necessity – and generally also one of the first things people notice when they walk into a bedroom. Therefore, they need to fulfil two mayor roles: they need to provide adequate storage and complement the existing décor by being attractive focal points.

Those lucky (or unlucky, depending on personal preference) enough to have only free-standing cupboards have a vast array of choices when it comes to style, colour, shape and size. Free-standing cupboards are also a decorator's favourite tool to add to the overall style of the bedroom – think sleek modern cupboards with sandblasted inlays and brushed metals knobs, imposing and oversized old-fashioned armoires decorated with delicate paint effects, or intricately carved Indonesian examples for an Eastern-inspired space.

Cupboard makeover

Tired of your less-than-stunning built-in cupboards? Change them (without spending too much money) by using any one of these quick makeover tricks.

Rehang the doors

Start by checking that the doors hang evenly, and adjust the hinges accordingly. Replace faulty hinges.

New handles

A change of handles or knobs will instantly update cupboard doors. Choose knobs that suit your decorating style: chic, shiny or brushed metal, crystal, mock old-fashioned or moulded plastic in various colours. Fill any remaining holes with woodfiller, leave to dry and sand smooth. If doors have a wooden veneer, opt for handles of the same size and shape as the initial ones, otherwise filled holes will remain visible.

tip

Should you decide to sell your house, stylish, good-quality built-in cupboards will add value to your home. Always repair cupboards and doors before placing your house on the market.

Paint appeal

If ordinary brown- or white-veneered melamine doors aren't your style, and replacing is not an option, simply paint them. Apply melamine primer to the doors and cupboard frame, inside and out. Follow with a good-quality paint. Replace the door handles to complement the new colour and you'll have new-looking cupboards in no time.

Add detail

Add three-dimentional detail by glueing lengths of wooden half-rounds, quadrant or halved bamboo to the front of cupboards in a frame-like shape. Paint the same colour as the rest of the cupboard door or a different colour for effect.

Take it off

If the cupboard doors are hideous, take them off and disguise the cupboard with a curtain. You will need to fit a curtain rod above the cupboard. Give it a modern edge by sewing a length of curtain tape with large metal eyelets onto plain canvas, and slide it onto a sleek metal rod.

New doors

There are various styles of doors with which to replace existing cupboard doors. Ordinary ones include melamine, PVC post-formed and semi-solid options. The more expensive options are semi-solid and solid wood options with interesting sandblasted glass and inlay detail.

All the options

Plain melamine panel doors are the most inexpensive option. They come in a variety of surface and edge finishes and are really very good value for money. PVC postformed and foil-wrapped doors have postformed (half-rounded) vertical edges that create clean and tidy lines. Some doors also have a slight wood-grain effect that prevents scratching and surface damage.

Ready-to-fit Supawood doors (the inside surface is generally finished in white melamine, the outside surface in a plain or moulded design) are ideal for paint or paint technique finishes. They are highly suitable for homeowners who want to upgrade existing cupboards. Semi-solid frame doors are made from ply-wood or chipboard (on a frame of MDF or solid wood). They are available in different designs ranging from a traditional five-piece construction, to some really exciting patented designs. They come in a variety of woodsand veneers, including pine, oak, maple, beech and cherry. Solid wooden doors are made from solid timber only, and are the most expensive option. They are also available in various designs, as well as types of wood.

All new

If the cupboard structure is coming apart, it is time for a complete overhaul. If the doors have recently been replaced, salvage them and simply have a similar but new frame built.

Creating space

The insides of existing cupboards aren't always suited to specific needs and often valuable space is wasted. There are several ways in which to overcome this problem.

◀ Wire storage. Handy wire units are made to fit inside existing bedroom cupboards. The baskets are available in various sizes and make excellent use of available space. The metal shelves and rails enable you to arrange the inside of your cupboard to suit your needs.

◀ Add and divide. Add a shoe-rail below hanging space to store shoes. Or lower the clothes rail and add a shelf above it for the same purpose. Also, add extra shelves where shelf openings are very wide so that you have a couple of smaller stacks of clothing rather than one large, very unmanageable pile.

◀ Remodel. Do you have an unused nook in the centre of a row of built-in cupboards? Better use this valuable space by taking out the existing shelf and adding a number of similar ones. Space them far enough apart (from the ceiling to the floor) to fit a couple of wicker baskets. Label the baskets so that you will be able to see at a glance where everything is or where something must be stored.

◀ Suspend. Twist hooks into the insides of doors and hang belts, jewellery, bags and any other small accessories, thus storing it all neatly and out of sight.

Top right Open-canvas storage, hooked onto a metal rail, is ideal when space is at a premium.
Right Mobile trollies are great for keeping clutter off the floor. They are especially useful in children's bedrooms.

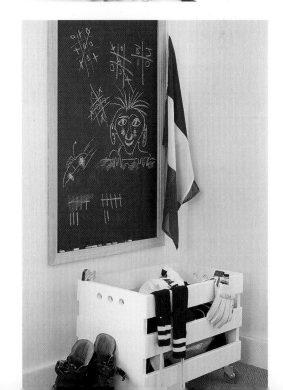

Children's bedrooms

Children's bedrooms can be loads of fun to decorate – but also time-consuming and costly. There are, however, ways and means with which to create the ideal room without breaking the bank. Good planning is essential, because a well-planned room will simply evolve into a new one as the little one grows older – avoiding a complete overhaul every few years.

Age

Initially, a baby needs only a place to sleep and a surface upon which to be changed. As they grow, various colours and other stimuli should be introduced to help with their development. Toddlers are more mobile and will need space in which to play, discover and make a mess. Use washable, stain-resistant paint on walls and a floorcovering that is easy to clean, yet yielding and soft enough to play on. A loose, washable rug is a good call – ensure that it has a non-slip coating underneath to prevent falls and slips.

As children reach school-going age, a desk and suitable chairs become necessary for doing homework. They will also need adequate personal space in which to relax.

tip

Once your children start developing their own preferences, include them in the decision-making process when you decorate their rooms – this will give them a very satisfying sense of ownership.

Be practical

If you plan to have another child soon after your first, consider keeping the nursery unchanged – it will save both money and effort. If needs be, change an accessory or two to make the room a little different, buy new curtains or a new rug.

Decorating schemes and themes

Parents are often wary of decorating according to themes, because of the relatively short lifespan of TV and movie heroes. Compensate for this and opt for a more general theme (such as the sea or circus), keeping the room fairly basic. Use only one or two paint colours and set the scene using different themed accessories. Adding lampshades, a loose rug and wall or window decals will be an effective and affordable way to go about it. Because there is a growing number of home stores, themed accessories are readily available and much more affordable than before. Create added interest on walls by painting one focal wall in a different colour, or divide the wall horizontally and paint the two parts different colours. You could also use various pictures and posters to add colour, or you could hang decorations from the ceiling to add colour and interest, while keeping the wall a single colour.

Furniture

There is a wonderful array of very tempting furniture with which to decorate children's rooms. But do beware of costly pieces that might not be popular in a few years (or even months). Rather choose furniture that can be converted or adapted as the child grows older, for example, a cot with removable sides is the perfect little bed for older toddlers.

Don't fall into the trap of thinking that everything must be new. Have a look at your existing furniture and customise a piece to suit a function. A table or desk can easily be adapted and used as a changing station. Simply add wooden edging to hold the mattress in place and attach a towel rail to the front or the side. Revamp an old shelf with a splash of paint, and mount it over the table or desk to store all the little one's lotions and potions. Transform an ordinary bed with a neat cover and use it as a stylish divan that will provide Mom and Dad with a comfortable resting place at night.

Opposite Bold graphic shapes in bright colours are perfect for adventurous young boys' room.

Above Nurseries need not be filled with soft, frilly bits.
Use graphics and striking lines for a more contemporary look.

Provide kiddie-sized furniture to create a play area that will keep toddlers entertained. Colourful plastic pieces (especially stackable furniture) are easy to keep clean, affordable and very durable.

For school-going children, provide enough space for books, projects, research books, as well as computers, trophies and other memorabilia. Due to the number of extramural activities in which they are involved, children generally need more storage space than adults. Prevent clutter and ensure tidier rooms by providing clever storage solutions such as mobile drawers (for under beds), wire storage systems for cupboards, adequate shelf space, loads of wall-mounted hooks and sturdy plastic storage boxes for all the little extras.

Bunk beds (of wood or metal) are ideal where space is limited, or where children share a room. Invest in two sets of bunk beds and you'll never run out of sleeping space when friends sleep over. An ordinary bed can be fixed onto sturdy poles, and bolted to a wall to create space underneath for a desk and cupboards. A number of space-saving combinations of bunk beds, desks and shelves are also available – perfect for growing children. Beds that are higher than normal, and placed over a base with sturdy drawers, are practical for storing toys, clothes or extra bedding, and very suitable for small, single rooms.

Flooring

Opt for easy-to-clean, hard-wearing floors. Wood and linoleum are good examples and can be softened by adding a machine-washable rug or two. Tiled floors are very unyielding and should preferably be covered with a large soft rug. They also tend to be cold during winter. Carpets are high-maintenance flooring in very young children's rooms and should preferably be hard-wearing, washable and stain resistant.

Wooden floors

Seal the boards with a good quality sealant and place protectors under moveable furniture to prevent scratches. A loose rug for playtime is a good idea – place a rubberised lining underneath it to prevent slipping.

Carpeting

Wall-to-wall carpeting or a room-sized rug, provides children with a comfortable, soft surface on which to play. A carpet with a low, densely packed pile is easy to clean, strong and durable. A cut-pile carpet with a frieze twist is also a good option – it hides dirt, has a pebbly, informal look, and is suitable for high-traffic areas.

Tiles

Ceramic and natural tiles can be quite cold and are hard under-foot – soften and warm the room by putting down a big, thick rug with a non-slip layer underneath.

Sponge tiles

Sponge tiling is a fun way to stimulate young minds. These tiles fit together like a jigsaw puzzle to form a soft, durable surface, and are simply placed over existing flooring. (They are available at most hypermarkets and large retailers.) They do, however, have a limited lifespan, as children outgrow them at a certain age, and they don't last long.

Walls

Invest in good quality, durable, washable and stain-resistant paint. Paint the lower part of the wall with durable enamel paint – good quality water-based enamel paint will not chip or scratch easily. Specially formulated paint specifically for children's rooms is available as well. It is washable, fast-drying, and odourless – the main idea being that the child will be able to sleep in the room the very same evening of the morning that it was painted.

Windows

In nurseries, thick blinds or blackout linings on curtains will ensure that baby sleeps undisturbed during the day. Soft light-textured curtaining will provide privacy for parents during feeding times, and when baby is awake. For toddlers and older kids, make sure that rooms receive enough sunlight during the day. Provide heavy curtaining or blinds for privacy and darkness at night. Safety clips on windows or burglar bars will prevent little ones from climbing or falling out of a window.

Lighting

Provide ample ambient lighting. Built-in down-lights are a good idea. Then the little one's antics won't dislodge, pull down or break them easily. They provide crisp, white light and create a starry effect on the ceiling – this could be further enhanced by painting silvery star-like shapes on the ceiling.

Avoid hanging fixtures, especially ones made from glass, because these are easily damaged or broken. Fine glass shards are difficult to remove from carpeting and can be very dangerous.

If a room is shared, provide separate night lights and study lamps for each occupant to prevent contention. Attach any trailing wires to the wall or skirting board and provide ample bedside space for lamps and other paraphernalia. If space is limited, opt for wall-mounted night lights, and study lamps that can be clipped onto tables, desks or shelves. Make sure that

light switches are within easy reach.

Avoid harsh, bright lights in the nursery that will hurt the baby's eyes, and wake them when they should still be sleeping. Rather place a lamp or night light high on the wall to cast a soft glow so parents can check up on the baby during the night.

It is advisable to provide a night light with a very low wattage if very young children are afraid of the dark. Touch-sensitive lights are also a good option – some of these can be wall-mounted right next to the little one's bed.

Provide adequate lighting in older children's rooms for activities such as arts and crafts, and homework at night.

Quick decorating tricks

◄ Update melamine cupboard doors with new handles or prime and paint to match the rest of the décor.
◄ Paint a blackboard panel on the lower half of one wall (or create a framed one) for children to draw and mess on.
◄ Buy plastic animals and tie them with string to the edges of lampshades or pin them to dado rails to match a farmyard or similar theme.
◄ Cut large, brightly coloured letters from felt or thin cardboard and attach to cupboard doors (out of children's reach) to use as a learning tool.
◄ Paint a road map or countryside scene on wooden floorboards for play inspiration.
◄ Decorate Chinese rice paper lanterns with fake flowers, stars, or fun elements to match a theme.
◄ String strands of non-flickering fairy lights around the room to add to a theme and make bedtime fun.

bathroom makeover

In the stress-filled world of today, the bathroom needs to be more than purely functional. It should also be a place in which you can escape from daily stresses and strains. The modern bathroom should be a place in which you can relax, while you cleanse both body and mind.

Decorating and designing a room in which so many functions combine is often quite a challenge and almost always a little expensive. If done correctly, however, it will add great value to your home. The concept of relaxation has become an all important feature in the bathroom and it is, therefore, important that this room be warm and welcoming, tranquil and serene.

If your bathroom isn't working for you at the moment, think about the things you would like to change. Is the towel rail impractically positioned, is there too little storage space, is the bath too close to the basin, or is the floorcovering unsightly?

With careful planning, your new design can smooth out all these headaches. Take a good look at the materials used in your bathroom. If the grout is stained, the floor often slippery and the window always steamed up, you'll know what to change.

Complete makeover (major budget)

Doing a major bathroom makeover is something you will probably only undertake once a decade, so be sure you do it right! It is essential that you plan everything carefully – before you rush out and buy cute little hand towels and a matching soap dispenser. Make sure that what you have planned will suit every member of the household. Also ensure that there will be adequate ventilation, provided either by an extractor fan or a window.

Most importantly – always use a qualified plumber!

Moving major fittings and pipes

There are some basic plumbing and building considerations to bear in mind when designing your new bathroom or when you're redesigning the present lay-out.

◄ Locate the water pipes.

◄ Don't move fittings too far from the soil stack. This will only create more work. You will probably need to raise the floor level to create a cavity for piping.

◄ If you plan to install a traditional steel or cast-iron bath, make sure the structure and flooring can take the weight of the bath, the water and you!

◄ Bathroom waste must be piped to the soil stack, which usually runs down the outside of your house.

◄ If you need to move fittings, it is easier if they are along the same wall as the soil stack. The further away they are, the more difficult it is to pipe away the waste, because the pipes must be angled downward for gravity to work. This isn't a problem in the case of a basin, which drains from waist height, but it is difficult with showers, where the water drains away from floor level.

◄ One of the most costly items to move is the toilet. This is because the waste must be piped through a 110 mm pipe.

◄ Hot- and cold-water pipes are easier to relocate.

◄ When you reroute pipes, bear in mind the construction of the floor.

◄ Always get expert advice on plumbing, electrical work and major structural alterations.

Choosing a bathroom style

There are many styles from which to choose and it is important that you choose one that will suit the whole household, as well as one that will complement the function of the room. Don't make any hasty decisions.

Classic

This bathroom is quite spacious, and the simple, yet classic fittings work well with natural materials that have a timeless appeal. The suite works as a backdrop for various decorative elements of your choice.

Contemporary

Use functional fittings with clean lines to achieve this look. Brushed stainless steel and polished oak work well. A modern bathroom often has lots of storage space – with both closed units and open shelving.

The suite

You're likely to keep the suite for many years, so don't choose something that you might tire of within a year or two. Your best bet would be to select classic shapes in neutral white. You can always experiment with the walls, flooring and accessories, which are much easier to replace.

tips

◄ A water leak in your bathroom will cause ugly stains or rust marks. Make sure that the pipes are not damaged and that there are no leaking taps adding to the problem. If there are problems, these should be solved, before you start removing the stains.

◄ Plan your bathroom in such a way that there is enough room for a standard mirror, an essential that no bathroom should be without.

Opposite The simple colours and smooth clean lines give this bathroom a very contemporary feel

Plan the perfect lay-out

Draw a scale plan of your bathroom. Include the windows
and the position of hot and cold pipes, drains, shaver sockets
and lights. Take into account the height of the windows,
and any obstacles such as a sloping roof.

Make cut-outs of all the fittings you would like and move
them around until you find the best arrangement. Work out
where you'd like the towel rails and shelves.

If space is very limited, opt for a shower instead of a bath,
or install a shorter bath. You can (if your budget allows) also
consider using space from the room next door by moving
the dividing wall (see page 56).

Each bathroom fitting needs a certain amount of space
around it, for example, to allow room for movement when
you're standing at the washbasin, or room to dry off once
you've stepped out of the bath.

Make cut-outs of all the extras in your bathroom, such
as laundry baskets and storage units. Move the cut-outs around
until you find the best lay-out. Indicate on your plan the
position of any extras such as shaving sockets, mirrors or lights.

A wet room

In a small en-suite bathroom, or anywhere you just need
an uncomplicated shower area, a wet room with no bath is
a great alternative.

In a wet room, the drainage hole is set into the floor, so
there is no need for a conventional shower tray, cramped little
enclosure or a clingy plastic shower curtain. The walls and
floor are usually tiled, and the floor is sloped slightly
towards the drain.

The installation of a wet room can be quite expensive – the
room must be fully lined to make it waterproof, and it
might also be necessary to raise the floor for to ensure
adequate drainage.

Consult your plumber and builder first. And keep in mind
that a wet room may only be practical on a ground floor. You
will also need to plan the lay-out carefully, making sure that
the basin and toilet aren't constantly splashed with water.

Non-slip floorcovering is absolutely essential.

tips

◄ To prevent the entire bathroom from getting soaked, consider using a circular shower curtain rail or install a solid
glass panel on one side.

◄ A wet room should not be the only bathroom in the
house. If ever you decide to sell your home, it may not be
such an attractive feature to a family with young children
who will, in all likelihood, prefer a conventional family bathroom with bath.

Above Wet rooms are perfect for small spaces. Position the shower such
that your basin and toilet aren't constantly splashed with water.

Our house: THE BATHROOM

before

The main bathroom was cold and uninviting, and also one of the most unattractive rooms in the house. The tiles made the room appear extremely dark, and a corner cupboard and shelf disturbed the balance within the room. The sash window was rotten, and the ceiling was coming apart. If that wasn't enough, the visible plumbing further marred the appearance of the room. To top it all, the toilet was clearly visible from the kitchen.

after

We gutted the room, but kept the toilet and the bath, because we liked the Victorian design. We moved the bath closer to the wall to create more space between the bath and basin. Sandstone tiles were used on the floor. The walls and the outside of the bath, were painted with Velvaglo. All the fittings were replaced with an elegant Victorian range, and we installed a nickel double towel rail, a glass and nickel shelf, a toilet roll holder and a soap dish. We also installed a new washbasin and pedestal. The dreary view from the sash window onto the small backyard and concrete wall was disguised using window film, which gave the window a lovely sandblasted-glass effect.

Storage

Every bathroom needs adequate storage space. There are few things as unglamorous and unsightly as cleaning detergents, toiletries and tubes of toothpaste that are out on display. The size of your bathroom will determine your storage options.

Clear the clutter

Storage is the key to style and comfort, even in the tiniest en-suite bathroom. Make sure you have enough space to stash towels and toiletries.

Keep in mind that towels need to be within easy reach of the bath, basin and shower. Towel hooks behind a door or a wall-mounted peg rail will work well.

Cabinets

Built-in cupboards are ideal where space is limited. Install them at the end of the bath or above the toilet. Choose a built-in unit with deep shelves for stacking towels, and storing toilet paper, accessories and any other vanity products.

Free-standing cupboards work well in a period-style room that has lots of space. Choose luxurious materials such as rich, dark wood and marble to complement the traditional feel.

If you have a wet room, enclosed storage is essential to protect everything from splashes. Opt for cabinets rather than open shelves, and use water-resistant materials.

Shelves

Choose shallow open shelves of glass, perspex or metal to store those items you like to put on display. Make use of dead wall space above the toilet for a slim shelf unit to store extra toilet rolls and air-freshener.

Don't forget to leave enough space for you to be able to open the cistern lid for maintenance and other purposes.

Baskets and other options

Baskets come in all shapes and sizes and are available in most furniture and home stores. Use them to store small items, and use bigger baskets for used towels and other laundry.

If space and budget allow, invest in a mobile trolley that you can move from the bath to the basin.

Shower rack

In the shower you will need a unit to store soap, shampoo, conditioner, etc. Here you can choose between wall-mounted racks or built-in ledges. Corner units take up less space and are available in chrome and plastic. A shower caddy is also useful.

tip

Store medicines and harmful cleaning agents well out of the reach of children, preferably in a secure cabinet that can be kept locked at all times.

cleaning tips

◄ If there is lime scale in the toilet bowl, clean it with a lime scale remover that has a gel con sistency, which will make it stick to the sides of the bowl. If there are heavy deposits, empty the water from the bowl – bail the water out or tie up the float-operated inlet valve (ball cock), and flush the toilet. Don't leave toilet cleaner in contact with the surface longer than the recommended time. It will penetrate cracks in the glaze and cause discolouration.

◄ If you have an acrylic bath, clean it after each use to prevent a build-up of dirt. Use an all-purpose cleaning agent, and use a nylon brush on stubborn marks. Fine scratches can be removed by rubbing gently with a metal polish, then cleaned as above.

◄ Use a gel cleaner and an old toothbrush to dislodge stubborn deposits of lime scale around taps and drains.

◄ Clean the shower screen with a weak solution of washing-up liquid. If you have a folding shower screen, pay particular attention to the hinge mechanism, which tends to be a dirt trap.

◄ To remove mildew from the shower curtain, scrub with a solution of 20 ml household bleach to 5 litres water. Rinse it thoroughly.

Opposite left Closed cupboards are perfect for storing bathroom essentials that you'd rather not put on display.
Opposite right This small, functional workbench provides loads of storage space for towels and bath-time products.
Left Narrow, old-fashioned display cabinets are ideal for larger bathrooms that need extra storage space.

Fittings and suites

A bathroom shouldn't have to be redecorated very often, so keep this in mind when you choose the fittings and when you decide upon a colour. Keep it simple and bear in mind that you can always jazz it up with funky and colourful accessories.

Baths

Baths are available in acrylic, steel or cast-iron, and come in a variety of shapes and sizes, from conventional to corner, and free-standing designs. Acrylic is lightweight and warm to the touch. Although tough enough to withstand daily wear and tear, it can be damaged by harsh chemicals, as well as essential oils. Cast-iron baths are very heavy, so your floor may need to be reinforced. Steel baths have the solid feel of cast-iron, without the added weight; they have an enamel finish that may chip.

Basins

Basins are available in pedestal, wall-mounted and counter-top styles. Pedestals have a classic look, but there is a lot to clean. Wall-mounted basins look tidy as the plumbing is concealed behind the wall and there is no pedestal that clutters the floor.

A counter-top style basin can be supported by a cupboard that has space for storage. Two basins, set into a worktop, is another design that has become very popular.

Taps

There is a wide range of taps available. When choosing taps for your bathroom, always narrow down the choice to those fittings that are compatible with your suite.

Taps come in either chrome- and gold-plate effects or solid plate. The choice of waste outlet should complement the tap design. Conventional design taps work well in almost any style of bathroom. You can buy reproductions, or go for original reconditioned fittings. Be sure to check that they are compatible with your existing plumbing.

Below left and centre All bathrooms need ample hanging space for towels. Use double rails if space is limited.
Below right and opposite Fixtures with clean, classic lines will suit almost any bathroom. Choose a style that will outlast any trend.

Shower heads

There are a few styles from which you can choose:

Mixer showers

Mixer showers are the most commonly used type of shower. Like a mixer tap, you control the temperature of the water from central water outlet by adjusting the hot and cold taps. The pressure may not be sufficient for a good shower if you have a gravity-fed system, or if you have a combi-boiler, and the mains pressure is not very high. Thermostatic versions are more expensive, but they regulate the water temperature and prevent extreme fluctuations. They will, for example, prevent the water from becoming scalding hot when someone flushes the toilet while you're in the shower!

Power showers

Power showers are mixer showers that have a pump attached. They're great for quick, invigorating showers, as long as the hot-water cylinder and cold-water tank can cope. A pump cannot be attached to the mains supply, so power showers can only be used with gravity-fed systems. This means the water tank must be situated at least one metre above the shower for it to be able to provide the required water pressure. An extra pump can be installed to create a power shower.

Electric showers

These are fed by mains water that's instantly heated by a heater within the shower unit. The flow rate depends on how powerful the unit is and on the temperature of the incoming water. For example, the flow will be slower in winter because the cold, incoming water will take longer to heat up. If the mains pressure is not high enough, install a pump system that feeds from the cold-water tank. Electric showers are fairly inexpensive and easy to install. In addition, you won't need to have a full tank of hot water ready every time you want to take a shower.

Shower units

Free-standing shower units are usually available in these four shapes: square, rectangle, corner unit and quadrant (a corner unit with a curved front edge). Think about the space around the shower – is there room for doors that swing outwards? In a small room, try an enclosure with doors that fold inwards, or saloon doors (half-width doors) that swing outwards. A pivot-door enclosure is perfect for a corner shower, since the doors on each side slide back from the front corner.

Towel rails

Choose towel rails, holders and accessories that form a set. Chrome is a popular choice, while more traditional rails are suitable in a classic bathroom design. Heated towel rails are perfect for those cold winter mornings.

Toilets

The most commonly used toilets are close-coupled systems, that is, the bowl and the cistern are part of the same neat unit. Semi-close-coupled units look the same but cost less. The old-fashioned units that have a separate low- or high-level cistern are still available, however, and will look perfect in a Victorian-style bathroom. Back-to-wall toilets have the cistern concealed behind a wall, and wall-hung versions are completely suspended from the wall, with no pedestal on the floor. Bidet designs include – overrim supply, rim supply, and a rim supply with ascending spray. Less stringent regulations apply to fitting overrim supply bidets.

Unusual fittings

If you're looking for unusual bathroom fittings, be on the lookout for reclaimed materials. Original period baths, basins and taps can add a huge amount of character to your bathroom. If you find a cast-iron bath with a damaged surface, don't let that put you off. It can very easily be re-enamelled (see page 113) or relined with perspex, in much the same way as a modern acrylic bath.

Surfaces

While you can't always do exactly as you please with the lay-out of your bathroom, you can be as creative as you like with the decoration of the walls. Choose finishes that suit your style.

Tiles

Tiles are ideal for a waterproof splashback around the basin and the bath. They come in a variety of colours and shapes to suit any style and budget. If necessary, they may even be fixed over old tiles.

When laying tiles, keep in mind that the grouting has a huge effect on their finished appearance. Choose a similar tone that blends with the tiles, or for fun, choose a contrasting shade to create an unusual effect.

Paint

Make sure you use a specially formulated bathroom paint that's resistant to damp, fungal growth and mildew. This will save you a lot of effort and expense in the long run.

Use a special undercoat to kill existing mould and cover any stains. This will ensure that old mould doesn't surface later. There are various brands on the market, so consult your local paint supplier, and then follow the manufacturer's instructions on the tin.

Usually, one application of undercoat is applied, and takes about 45 minutes to dry completely (naturally, the undercoating won't be necessary in a brand-new bathroom).

Next, for a more permanent solution, apply mildew-proof bathroom paint. The paint doesn't actually kill mildew, but it contains a special resin that prevents regrowth.

Of course, before you paint anything, make sure that all surfaces have been thoroughly cleaned and that everything that isn't going to be painted is well protected. Most importantly of all, ensure that the room is well ventilated.

Plaster

Any plastered bathroom walls should be covered in mould-resistant matt paint.

Tongue-and-groove panelling

Tongue-and-groove panelling has a warm and inviting quality, and is particularly suited to older homes where it adds a little extra charm. It is a very attractive and cost-effective way of transforming bathroom walls.

Tongue-and-groove panelling will cover an uneven surface, and it can be painted (with a hard-wearing, oil-based paint), varnished or stained. To install tongue-and-groove panelling, you first need to build a wooden framework to which to attach the boards.

Other alternatives

There are various brands of wallpaper available that can withstand the humid bathroom atmosphere. However, they are usually also the more expensive alternative.

tips

◀ Tiling an entire wall can be expensive. If you need to cut costs, tile only the splashbacks and the shower area.

◀ Before making any final decisions. Ask for sample tiles to take home. It will be much easier for you to make the right decisions if you can view the tiles within the relevant context.

◀ Mosaic tiles are perfect for splashbacks and give a fresh contemporary feel.

◀ Use tiles of two different sizes, mix and match, and create an individual look.

◀ Glass art tiles, used as basin splashbacks, will add glamour to your bathroom.

◀ To keep your bathroom free of harmful bacteria, use anti-bacterial grouts and sealants. They combat mould, mildew and bacteria.

◀ If mould has formed on tile grouting, clean it with an old toothbrush and a solution made up of one part bleach to four parts water.

◀ Never use lime-scale remover on enamel-coated baths. Instead, use neat washing-up liquid, and a soft plastic scourer.

Floors

If the current tiles don't suit your style, lay new tiles directly onto the old ones. Carpets are never a good idea in the bathroom, as they can become quite soggy and smelly. Tiles and terrazzo are popular. As is rubber flooring, which is waterproof, non-slip and warm under-foot. Bare floorboards look good, but it is difficult to seal the gaps between the boards to make them watertight. A laminate or hardwood floor that's been specifically designed for the bathroom is ideal. Also, consider vinyl. It is relatively inexpensive, watertight and comes in a variety of styles and colours.

Below Mosaic tiles are a bathroom basic that will never date. Use them selectively for splashbacks or around a bath. Balance bright tiles by using a soft-coloured paint on the remaining walls.

re-enamelling a bath

Enamel baths, although they're hard-wearing, their coating often chips or stains. Should this happen, you can either have your bath professionally re-enamelled, or do the job yourself. Use a proprietary re-enamelling kit (they are available at most hardware stores).

you will need:

- ✓ Masking tape and plastic covering
- ✓ Proprietary re-enamelling kit
- ✓ Paintbrush
- ✓ Paint roller and tray
- ✓ Gloves

how to:

Clean the bath with a mild detergent and leave to dry. Cover the taps and water outlets with masking tape and plastic covering (bags). Clean the bath with the cleaner and sponge supplied in the kit, rinse and leave to dry. Sand the surface with fine-grade abrasive paper. Rinse the bath with warm water, and leave to dry. In most cases you will have to mix the hardener with the coating before you apply it to the surface (follow the manufacturer's guidelines). Use a paint-brush on the areas around the outlets and taps. Pour some of the coating mixture into a roller tray. Apply the coating as evenly as possible with the paint roller. When it is dry, apply a second coat. Try to cover the roller marks to get an even fin-ish. It is best to use different roller sleeves for each coating otherwise you will get a rough finish.

tip
The bathroom must be well ventilated when you do this job as the fumes can be very overpowering.

step-by-step: **dry-wall**

You can change the appearance of a bathroom by disguising aspects that don't suit the look you're trying to create. One of the most cost-effective disguises is a dry-wall installation. Use it to conceal an exposed geyser or even exposed pipes beneath the basin. Here a bathroom toilet is concealed by building a small 120-cm wall, using easy-to-install Rhinoboard.

You will need:

- ✓ 12.5 mm moisture-resistant Rhinoboard
- ✓ RhinoTape
- ✓ RhinoLite plaster or cretestone
- ✓ RhinoGlide or RhinoJointfiller
- ✓ Dry-wall studs
- ✓ Tape measure (for setting out)
- ✓ Plumb bob (for aligning top and bottom tracks)
- ✓ Chalk line (for marking floor tracks, etc.)
- ✓ Spirit level
- ✓ Hacksaw or tin snips (for cutting studs and tracks to the required lengths)
- ✓ Carpet knife and spare blades (for cutting the RhinoBoard)
- ✓ Straight edge (for cutting RhinoBoard)
- ✓ Ultrasteel floor track

Other hand tools:

- ✓ Electric hand drill
- ✓ Pop-rivet gun
- ✓ Screwdriver
- ✓ Dry-wall gun or dry-wall screw adapter
- ✓ Hammer

create the look

How to:

1. On the floor, mark the position where the RhinoBoard is required.
2. Lay the Ultrasteel floor track according to your plan. Notch one side of the track section in small pie-sliced segments, at regular intervals. Fix the track using the standard RhinoBoard recommendations. Do the top and the bottom at the same time. It is advisable to check that all framework is straight and true at this point. It's a lot easier to rectify mistakes now, rather than after the wall is finished.
3. Attach 12.5 mm RhinoBoard with dry-wall studs. The studs should be installed at 400 mm centres.
4. Complete the wall by fixing another 12.5 mm sheet of RhinoBoard to the other side of the frame.

5. Place RhinoTape over the joints. Apply two layers of RhinoJointfiller or RhinoGlide and lightly sand down the joints. Fibre tape should be applied to all joints and the surface of the wall skimmed with a coat of RhinoLite plaster.
6. After the RhinoLite plaster has dried completely, decorate in your preferred manner.

tip
Before painting your dry wall, make sure it's dust-free. Use a good-quality water-based emulsion or acrylic paint as undercoating. But don't ever use oil or solvent-based under-coats. Alternatively, cover your dry wall with vinyl tiles.

electricity in bathrooms

All electrical work must be done by a qualified electrician. Light-bulb fittings must have covers to prevent electrocution. Fittings must be covered if they are likely to get wet. The only sockets you should ever have in a bathroom or a wet room are shaving sockets, which have a very low cut-out threshold to prevent electrocution. Major electrical appliances such as washing machines, tumble dryers and wall-mounted heaters must be wired to a sealed socket and out of reach of anyone using water.

Safety tips
Light switches must be outside the room, or operated by a string pull from inside. Thermostatic taps are a good idea, because they regulate the temperature and thus protect against scalding. If you choose floor tiles, make sure they are non-slip, and if you have a shower over the bath, fit a non-slip mat, or bath surface that provides better grip.

Finishing touches

Colour scheme

The colour of the bathroom suite (bath, washbasin, etc.) will determine your colour scheme. White is the most versatile. Dark-coloured fittings show marks more easily. Victorian baths suit the style of most older homes and there are many new and more affordable versions on the market. Plain plastered and screed walls, and slate tiles in natural, earthy colours and textures are very popular for bathroom décor. Select soothing colours in muted tones to create the desired effect. Use complementary colours for accents.

Windows

With all the moisture generated in a bathroom, a simple window treatment is the best option. Roller and Roman blinds can be made up in almost any colour or pattern, and wooden slatted blinds create a calm, natural feel. In a small bathroom you might want to forgo curtains and blinds altogether, and maintain privacy with etched windows. Replace the glass or spray the window with a glass-etch spray, available at selected hardware stores.

Lights

Soft, ambient lighting can be provided by a central light fitting, or halogen down-lights. Brighter task lighting will be needed around the mirror for shaving and applying make-up. Light bulbs should be enclosed with glass or plastic shades, or fixed into light fittings that are covered with plastic insulating shrouds that keep moisture away.

Candles

Candlelight is a great way to create mood and ambience. In the bathroom it is relaxing and invigorating. Always be candle-safe.

Great makeover tips

Link the décor in an en-suite bedroom and bathroom to create flow. The rooms need not be identical – simply repeat a certain colour, details or pattern to create a visually larger space.

If possible, remove the door between the two rooms and use soft, sheer fabric as a screen, or hang a gauze curtain in the doorway. You could also leave it completely open.

◄ Create privacy as well as impact by adding sheets of perspex or white sticky-backed plastic to the lower part of windows.

◄ A mirror will bounce light around.

◄ Clutter creates negative energy and gives the bathroom an untidy appearance. Store it or throw it away.

◄ When not in use, keep the toilet seat down and prevent your luck with money from being flushed away!

◄ Use calming shades in the bathroom such as aqua blue, light green, lilac and natural tones.

◄ Make sure that the lighting is ample, but not too harsh. It might be a good idea to install a dimmer switch.

◄ If the bathroom sink is stained and dirty, rub light stains with a freshly cut lemon and rub dark stains with a paste of borax and lemon juice.

◄ To freshen a drain, pour half a box of baking soda down the drain, then add half a cup of white vinegar. Cover the drain tightly for a few minutes and flush with cold water.

Opposite This antique mirror plays an important part in defining the bathroom's style.

cost-effective bathroom changes

You don't need to spend a fortune to modernise a bathroom, and you don't need to strip your bathroom completely to give it a brand-new look. The most cost-effective changes are small ones, such as replacing outdated light fixtures with modern ones, or fitting tongue-and-groove panelling to the lower part of the walls, or simply, tiling or painting over the existing tiles. Avoid repositioning the bathroom fixtures (the toilet, basin and bath or shower) as plumbing costs can be extremely high. Rather try to keep these in their original positions, especially the toilet. Otherwise, look around for chipped or stained baths, basins or tiles that have been resurfaced in the colour of your choice. Buy quality fittings or tiles that have tiny flaws and you might be able to work around the flaws cleverly and save quite a bit of money. You can save both money and space by forgoing a full vanity table. Instead, opt for a basin, hung against the wall, and a very plain wall shelf.

Other cost-effective bathroom changes include:
- replacing counter tops and flooring with inexpensive tiles
- re-enamelling the bath and basin
- regrouting wall tiles
- repainting the ceiling and untiled walls in white or another light colour
- installing a large mirror above the vanity unit
- replacing taps, light fittings and towel rails with new ones.

Adding an extension to your house will not only provide you with the extra space you need, but can add considerable value to your home. For your extension to be a success, it needs to be done with careful thought and thorough planning. A little patience, too, is going to go a long way.

extensions

Red tape

Any building plans that either change or add to the existing structure of you home, will need to be approved by your local municipality. If you fail to comply with the regulations they have set out, you can expect to be charged a rather stiff fine – every single day that you build without the proper consent.

If you're planning renovations that will change the function of a room or the function of your entire house (for example, turning it into a guest house), you will need municipal approval as well. This is because these changes may impinge upon the structural strength of the building, and could affect health and fire regulations. When all the construction work has been completed, the municipality has to inspect the property in order to provide you with a certificate of occupation.

Before commissioning any plans or setting your heart on adding a conservatory to your house, find out exactly when it was built. If it was built more than 50 years ago, any proposed changes will need to be approved by the Provincial Heritage Resources Agency. Once the agency has approved your plans, you will still need to apply for municipal approval before you can start any construction work.

Don't jump the gun

Before making any structural changes to your new home, ensure that the transfer has successfully been processed, or ask for written consent from the previous owner. Even with this consent, however, you will be well advised to wait until the sale has been finalised. Rather safe than sorry, it is better to do everything by the book.

Set a realistic budget

Plan carefully and make sure your budget will cover all possible eventualities. Talk to people who have recently done home extensions and ask them about any hidden costs that you might not have catered for in your budget. Be realistic about whether you can afford to make the proposed changes. Are you going overboard? Or are you not maximising the full potential of your property? Will these changes fit in with your lifestyle, both present and future? Or are you proposing changes that will only serve your purposes a year or two? Think about a loan repayment-plan and set yourself realistic goals. Make sure that your budget has some flexibility – enough for you to be covered in case of an emergency, but not enough for you to break the bank.

Think it through

Take a stroll around the house and in the garden. Make a mental note of changes you think would be possible and those that you would like to see made. A two-dimensional sketch of your home will be very useful in helping you to see what your proposed changes could look like, and whether or not they are actually physically possible.

When thinking about renovating or remodelling your home, always be aware of the original style of the house. Where possible, keep to this style and don't remove original features like wooden floors or a fireplace. Change is good, and often unavoidable, but don't start making changes just for the sake of it. When you set about renovating your period home, the last thing you want is to end up with a modern monstrosity.

Keep the style of the house in mind when you consider exterior or interior changes. Think about small changes that will successfully retain the style of the house, for example, a picket fence or the shape and size of your mailbox; or the colour and design of light switches and other interior fittings. Choose your paint wisely and don't stray too far from the colours that were popular during the era in which your house was built.

Below Make the most of existing space by converting an unused attic into a loft room.

Adding a room

A spacious place

Adding an extension to a living room or kitchen can completely transform the spaciousness of your home. Adding an extra bedroom, a guest bathroom or a study will add greatly to its function and value. The simplest and most inexpensive way to add a room to your home is by utilising unused space. You could do this with a simple loft conversion or you could decide to utilise unused garden space and build an additional room or two. Naturally, whatever you decide will depend on certain factors, for example, how much available space there is, and how much extra room you want.

Whether you're doing a loft conversion or building an extra room, make sure that the architecture blends well with the rest of the house and use the same trim, window and roofing detail. When building an extra room, consider giving it a raised or vaulted ceiling. This cost-effective little trick will make the room feel very spacious and can be complemented with skylights or large windows.

Make it worth your while

When it comes to remodelling, kitchens and bathrooms remain the all-time favourites. They add the most value to a property and are more likely to give you a return on your investment than any other home extension. Adding a second bathroom can also be profitable, especially if it makes use of much of the existing plumbing. This could, estate experts say, add at least twice the cost of the addition to the value of your home.

Another popular improvement that can add value is a loft conversion. Design plays an important part in this kind of conversion, so you will do well to ask an architect for advice.

Although it sounds simple enough, adding rooms to the top of a house is not always the best option. If the lower level turns out looking smaller than the upper level, your house is going to look top heavy and in danger of toppling over. In addition, if there is only one bathroom on the lower level, don't try and convert one of the extra rooms on the upper level into one – they are not suitable for this purpose.

Ask an expert

Adding a room to you house or remodelling your kitchen is no simple and easy task. It will be well worth your while to obtain the expert advice or services of an architect. It may cost a pretty penny, but in the long run, a job well done by a professional is still going to cost much less than a job poorly done by an over-ambitious novice. An architect will help you identify the hidden potential of your home and can suggest solutions to any structural problems you might have. He or she will also know all the relevant details about the municipal rules and regulations applicable to your home, and have the fun job of getting your renovation or building plans approved. Most importantly, an architect will (or should at least) stop you from making very expensive mistakes.

Some free advice

It is vitally important that your extension blends well with the rest of your house and that the workmanship looks neat and professional. An obvious extension or an extension that has poor quality workmanship, will add zero value to your home. In all likelihood, it will cause a considerable reduction in the value of your property.

Extensions should preferably be made only towards the back of the house. Avoid having to change the face of your home. Make sure that your extension is positioned in such a way that you can make full use of the sunlight it receives. You will want to have a little warmth in winter and cool areas in summer. Make the most of any potential views your extension might look out upon. And always consider whether the style and structure of the house will be suitable for the changes you intend to make.

An open-plan design is great for letting in maximum light and creating a feeling of spaciousness. But be careful that you don't knock down too many walls and create a cold and drafty room. Bring light into the room by using glass doors, or opt for large bay windows.

Be sure to set aside funds for the interior decoration of the extension, as well as for the general improvement of the other rooms in your home. A fresh coat of paint should do the trick.

Make it look professional. Start small, but use quality finishes. Don't try and do too much with too little money. It will ultimately only cost you even more.

And last, but certainly not least, don't be afraid of experimenting, finding and expressing your own style. This is your house, and you (and your family) are the ones whose needs it must meet. As long as you adhere to the basic guidelines and principles of building an extension, and as long as nothing you do decreases the value of your home, you are free to design and style and decorate as you wish. Only one word of caution though, make sure that, in the frenzy and excitement of building and decorating your new room, you do not lose track of your spending and end up overcapitalising.

Overcapitalising on your extension means that what started out as something that was going to add value to your home, has resulted in something that has only cost you more money.

Building basics

Planning, preparation, and doing everything by the book is going to save you a lot of time and trouble. The Master Builder and Allied Trades Association (MBA) suggest that you use only MBA members, as this will ensure that your dream project does not turn into a complete nightmare.

One of the most important things you have to do is to make a detailed list of everything you wish to have done and then to match this with your budget to determine what you realistically can achieve. Be specific. List the work, the specifications, the materials to be used and the quality of work finishes required. If quotes received are too high, reassess your requirements in line with your budget.

When choosing a contractor, you should ensure proof of insurances; registration with statutory bodies such as the bargaining councils (if applicable to the area), SARS, and the Workman's Compensation Fund.

Be aware. The newly promulgated Construction Regulations make the client/owner responsible for occupational health and safety on a building site and the penalties for non-compliance are severe. However, should you employ a professional builder, you will not be faced with this liability. MBA offices employ safety advisors who can assist you in this regard. They or any of the members of the Building Industries Federation of South Africa (BIFSA) can supply you with a list of their members, which will include contractors and specialist subcontractors for waterproofing, plumbing, painting, and so on.

A written contract between you and the contractor is absolutely necessary – copies of applicable contracts, approved by the Building Industries Federation of South Africa (BIFSA), are available from MBA offices in most main centres. When drawing up a contract, make sure that you and your contractor are in complete agreement regarding the start and completion date of the construction work. Do not set an unrealistic target date that could lead to an unnecessary dispute.

Ensure that the alterations do not negatively affect the structural integrity of the house. Many people insist on walls being knocked down without thinking about the consequences. In most such cases they have employed a contractor without the necessary expertise and knowledge to advise them properly, which may lead to major unnecessary expenses being incurred at a later stage.

You should ensure that you understand the full impact of the alteration, extension or other changes you wish to make. Always seek the advice of a structural engineer if you are uncertain of the implications of the addition, alteration or extension.

It is necessary to ensure that potential external problems are taken into account as well, for example, will your new extension prevent the rainwater drainage from following its natural course, or is the new roof slope of the addition going to affect the formerly wind-free courtyard or entertaining area?

During the construction phase, always obtain quotations for additional work, not covered in the contract, before this work is carried out. Failure to do this could lead to lengthy disputes and bitter arguments.

Once construction has commenced, avoid making any changes or additions to the original plan and contract. This could lead to great irritation and confusion, and to terrible mistakes being made. Not to mention the considerable additional costs this may incur.

Any garden, large or small, is a valuable asset to the home. It's a place to which you can retreat, in which you can play, entertain, or relax. Whether it's a small balcony or a huge backyard, make the most of your outdoor space, and bring nature a little closer to your home.

outdoor living

The South African climate is ideal for outdoor living and, as such, the garden has become a central part of the home. It is very flexible in terms of style and design, and if you understand the basics you can easily create a garden that is perfectly suited to your home and your lifestyle.

The style of your garden will be determined by a number of factors such as the style of your house, your needs, the climate of your region, the time you have available to maintain it, and the needs of your family. Planting and maintaining a garden is immensely rewarding. Even if you don't have green fingers, watching a tiny plant thrive and grow is an extremely gratifying experience.

Often the first thing a guest or potential buyer will notice, your garden needs to be neat and well maintained. A flowerbed or lay-out that no longer works for you, can easily be changed or updated. Hold on to your sense of fun and adventure, explore all the different design possibilities, and experiment with various flowers, shrubs and trees. Get your hands dirty!

Garden design and style

The basic principles of design are just as applicable in your garden as they are in your home. And choosing the right plants to complement the style of your garden is equally as important as choosing the right furniture to match the colour of your living-room walls.

When choosing a style for your garden, make sure it's one that will match the style of your house. A garden that contrasts starkly with the style of your house will look out of place, and be of no value to the visual appeal of your home. Browse through gardening books and magazines, look for ideas and inspiration. Find the perfect garden to suit your home.

Modern

Characteristically minimalist and simplistic, and comprised mostly of hard landscaping (features such as paving, ponds, trellis, gravel, timber decking, mirrors, rocks sculptures, etc.), the contemporary garden seldom has very many plants and almost never a lawn. The style is easily achieved and makes for a garden that requires very little maintenance.

Formal

Neat geometric lines and a perfect symmetrical design make the formal garden quite a wonder to behold (and uphold). It is made up of immaculately shaped and clipped hedges and topiary, perfect geometrical flowerbeds, and clearly defined pathways. The design requires near mathematical precision. Unless you're truly confident that you can successfully achieve this look on your own, ask a professional landscaper to assist you with the basic lay-out. This style of garden requires a fair share of maintenance and will look truly unsightly if unkempt. If you have your heart set on this style, but know you won''t have the time to properly maintain it, ask a gardening service to come around once a week.

Cottage

Informal and romantic, the cottage garden is filled with an abundance of flowers and fruit trees. Annuals and perennials in a wide variety of colours and textures, shapes and sizes, ensure that the garden is never bare and constantly changing. The style will suit most homes and is well loved by children. It does, however, require regular maintenance, and ideally, a constant and steady supply of flowering plants.

Japanese

The Japanese garden can be designed using a number of different elements and features. The more traditional Zen-like garden consists of raked sand, and specially chosen and placed rocks, which represent nature. The more contemporary Japanese garden uses these elements, and combines them with a number of other traditional Japanese garden styles, to create what is typically thought of as a Japanese garden today. Any combination of the following is used: sand and rocks, a koi pond or another suitable water feature, miniatures and moss, maples and bamboo, and gravel or pebbles. It is a tranquil garden that calls for simple, yet powerful, design.

Indigenous

This style of garden is sure to save you time and money. Not only are indigenous plants almost always being promoted by garden centres, but they require little maintenance and much less water than other plants. South Africa has such an amazingly diverse and beautiful array of flowers, shrubs and trees that it almost doesn't make sense to buy anything other than proudly South African plants!

Mediterranean

This style is best suited to gardens that have well-drained soil, and that lie within winter rainfall areas. It is a garden style that is fairly low in maintenance and quite easy to achieve. Gravel is often favoured over lawn (so it's not ideal for the kids); favourite trees include olive and lemon trees.

Opposite A private little nook in paradise. These lush green plants provide welcome shade in a tropical setting.

Gardening basics

If you plan to invest time, money and effort in your garden, it is worth investing in a comprehensive gardening manual. You can also obtain valuable advice from your local nursery.

Planning

Determine what you need from your garden, and how much time you can allow for gardening. Do you need a space for children to play, or simply an attractive entertainment area?

Draw an accurate plan of the site and mark boundaries and existing trees, shrubs and beds. Position activity areas (entertainment, washing line) and note the garden aspect, slope, and wind direction. Only after choosing the style, and setting out and landscaping the garden are plants added. Several factors will influence the style of garden and the type of plants you choose:

Budget

A landscaper is costly, but saves lots of time (and effort). Cut down on the cost and use a landscaper only for heavy preliminary work (split this into stages, if necessary).

Time

If you don't have lots of free time on your hands, don't choose a complicated design, nor a style that is high maintenance. Opt for a simple design and style, with plants that require very little regular care and maintenance.

Garden character

Make sure you know which parts of your garden are sun-drenched and which areas are mostly covered in shade. Choose the most suitable plants accordingly.

Soil type

Certain plants thrive in certain soils, and whither away in others. Avoid costly mistakes and take a soil sample to your local garden centre. They will be able to tell you what type of soil you have and how best to prepare it for your plants.

Wants

Do you want to spend hours in the garden tending to your plants? Or do you want to spend hours in the garden reading or relaxing? Decide what you ultimately want from your garden, and make your choices accordingly.

Choosing plants

Take time to find out which plants will do well in the different parts of your garden. A walk around your neighbourhood should give you a good idea of what would thrive in your area. Make a list of suitable plants, and then choose those that fit in with your chosen style. Be careful of impulse-buying when browsing at the nursery, and when in doubt, ask for advice or assistance.

Work with what you have

Giving an existing garden a makeover need not mean that you have to start from scratch. Unattractive trees and shrubs can be given a new lease on life with a proper feeding. Give them a new look with a thorough trim. Established trees and shrubs add maturity to any garden, and are too valuable to be removed without careful thought.

When moving into a new house, always try to find out as much information as possible about the established plants in the garden. It may be that the half-dead, dowdy-looking shrub in the corner gives a fantastic floral display in the spring – so know what you can safely pull out and throw away, and what you should try and nurse back to health as soon as possible!

Garden features

Water features, garden lights, and irrigation systems are permanent fixtures that may add value to your garden and home. Installing them may require some digging, so position them before you start planting.

Water features bring movement and light to the garden, instantly transforming their surrounds. Often serving as a focal point, some water features also produce lovely tranquil sounds. They come in a variety of shapes and sizes and there is a model and a make to suit every pocket. When budgeting and comparing prices, bear in mind that the larger water features often require a pump to filter the water, i.e. the running water will be a running cost, and the pump may need to be installed by a professional.

Lights that illuminate the exterior of your home are both decorative and a valuable part of security. Make sure that garden paths (especially the one leading up to the front door) are well lit.

An irrigation system will save both time and money when it comes to keeping your garden well watered, and it is well worth the initial outlay. Choose a garden lay-out that will remain reasonably static, in order to avoid having to move the irrigation pipes around at a later stage.

Pest-repelling summertime tips

◄ Parsley doesn't just go well with garlic, it's also a very effective pest repellent. Rub it on your face and hands. .

◄ Eating loads of Marmite before a hike in the bush is a sure-fire way of repelling insects. The Marmite smell will evaporate through your skin and deter any nasty critters.

◄ Lemon, eucalyptus and tea-tree oil all produce smells that repel insects. Sprinkle a few drops on your patio-table linen and keep your pool party insect-free.

◄ Flies bugging you? Slice a few lemons in half, stud them with cloves and place them in a bowl on your patio table.

◄ If ants are a problem, find the source of the invasion, and pour a kettle of hot water into the nest. Do not tackle a wasp nest in this way. They will attack! It is best to call pest control experts to do the job; the same applies for a beehive.

essential gardening tools

◄ **Lawnmower and edge-trimmer** (or weed-eater).

◄ **Broom:** essential to sweep away dirt, debris and leaves on outside decks, paving and concrete floors.

◄ **Hand tools:** more manageable than long-handled tools, small hand tools, such as a trowel and scoop are perfect for planting seedlings.

◄ **Pruning saw and goggles.**

◄ **Strong, waterproof gardening gloves.**

◄ **Dutch hoe:** the ideal tool for chipping weeds out of the garden with ease.

◄ **Hedge trimmers.**

◄ **Spade:** to dig, transport small amounts of soil, and to define garden beds and borders.

◄ **Secateurs:** perfect for pruning, and to take cuttings.

◄ **Rake:** an absolute must for gathering fallen leaves, lawn clippings and other loose garden debris.

◄ **Wheelbarrow:** make heavy loads lighter.

◄ **Garden fork:** to fracture soil.

◄ **Post-hole shovel:** just what the doctor ordered for moving mulch and compost.

◄ **Hose :** no garden can be without one. Don't water the garden and then leave your hose out in direct sunlight. This will cause the plastic to crack and deteriorate, and it will also be an open invitation to any passers-by to help themselves to your hose. If you're struggling with a hose that constantly buckles and twists, buy a hose roller for storage.

◄ **Sprayer/sprinkler head.**

Patios and pots

The patio is the perfect outdoor entertainment area. It creates a link between the home and the garden, and becomes an extension of the house itself. If you don't have a patio, invest in one! Patios are easy to design and lay out, and inexpensive to construct. You can choose from a variety of materials, ranging from traditional brick paving to a stately timber deck.

Planning and positioning

Decide where you want your patio to be situated and mark out the area. Observe the area over a couple of days and see if it's really practical. Ideally the site should be sunny but protected from wind and direct sun. Construct a canopy or use large outdoor umbrellas if your trees don't provide adequate shade. Position the patio so that it's easily accessible from the house, especially if you plan to eat and entertain outdoors. You might be carrying plates of food and drink up and down, and you need to make this as easy as possible. If you enjoy alfresco cooking, consider constructing a built-in braai.

Patio perfect

◀ Pay attention to proportion and consider the size of the materials you use. For example, flagstones might be too large and look out of proportion if they are used to cover a small area. Brick paving or a solid deck will be better options.

◀ A small space scattered with lots of small container plants, will only look cluttered and even smaller than it already is. Rather opt for one or two larger, yet striking, containers, and plant them with a colourful array of flowers.

◀ Tall plants can look really dramatic and be very effective in a small space where they draw the eye upwards.

◀ Limit your colour palette to just a few colours that work well together and create a stylish, harmonious feel.

◀ Make tall walls and fences appear less imposing with a painted trellis and a mix of climbers.

◀ Use beautifully planted hanging baskets to decorate the vertical space of your patio.

◀ Scented plants are a wonderful addition to any patio.

patio DIY

Construct a patio in a weekend using large cement pavers.
1. Clean the cement pavers: remove all grime and dirt.
2. Paint the pavers: use grey stoep/floor paint. Add a dash of black ochre powder to give the paint a more interesting appearance; leave to dry.
3. Prepare the site: remove all roots, and topsoil from the site (keep the topsoil aside for gardening later).
4. Level the ground: use white building sand, and cover with a waterproof plastic membrane. Plastic will deter weeds from growing in between the paving.
5. Lay the painted pavers: start in one corner, leaving a 3 to 5 cm space between them. Make sure the paving is level by checking it regularly with a spirit level.
6. Finish: spread gravel in between the pavers.

Container gardening

Planted with striking flowering annuals or topiary shrubs, containers add interest to and brighten up any space. Use potted plants for seasonal colour in the garden, or place potted herbs near the kitchen.

Make sure that the container isn't too small, and that the soil has been properly prepared. Soil should be well drained and rich in nutrients. Container plants require more regular and frequent watering than those planted in open ground, particularly in summer, when soil dries out quickly. Plants in hanging baskets may require watering twice daily, both morning and evening. Container plants also need to be given more nutrients and should be fed once every two weeks during growing season. Use a water-soluble organic fertiliser such as Nitrol or Seagro. Either apply with a watering can or put into a spritz bottle and apply as a foliar feed (spraying the foliage).

Opposite Treat your patio the same as you would any other room. Limit your palette to a few colours, and make sure plants, flowers and garden furniture all work well together.

you will need:

- ✓ paintable fibre-cement container
- ✓ black water-based paint
- ✓ paint brush
- ✓ rust paint
- ✓ rust activator

how to:

1. Thoroughly clean the container.
2. Apply one coat of black paint to the outside as well as up to where the pot will be filled on the inside. Allow to dry.
3. Apply one coat of rust paint to the exterior. Dab the paint on to achieve a stripy effect. The more layers you apply, the better the ageing effect will be.
4. Before the second coat has dried completely, dab on the activator.

Our house: THE COURTYARD

before

The grim backyard, with its pre-cast concrete walls and cement pavers, was gloomy and in desperate need of a revamp. The washing line and rubbish bins added to the neglected appearance. The previous owners hadn't

trimmed the tree, the creepers, or the vine, so it was overgrown and very shady. To top it all, there wasn't any kind of light to illuminate the area at night. We demolished the wall between the carpark and the backyard, and in doing so extended the patio by two metres. We repeated the design of the front boundary wall to create a flow with the rest of the garden.

after

We fitted a wall lantern above the doors leading to the patio, and on the side of the house, we fitted two eyelid bulkhead pathfinders. We lifted, cleaned, painted and spaced the existing concrete pavers and filled the gaps with gravel. With rocks from the front garden we created a water feature as focal point. We concentrated on a few plants, such as rosemary and lavender, planted directly in the soil for a low-maintenance patio garden. We clad the remaining Vibracrete wall with cement, painted it in a soft white, and layered it with wood lattice, which was painted in the same shade.

garages and carports

Don't rush into adding a garage if it's not going to blend well with the rest of your house and property. An obvious addition will only detract from the visual appeal of your home, and ultimately reduce the total value of your investment.

Adding value

A double garage adds value to your home and increases its resale potential. It not only provides security and protection for your vehicles, but also offers extra storage space. A double garage that leads directly into the main house will protect you and your shopping bags from the elements. However, make sure that the entrance into the house is secure and not an easy access point for burglars.

Make sure the garage is properly locked at all times, especially if you use it to store tools (burglars could use your own tools to break into your home). As an added safety precaution, consider installing an electric door, eliminating any need for you to get out of your car in the driveway or on the street.

Do it the right way

A garage is a permanent structure and must be built according to specific guidelines. Unless you're an expert, use a reputable builder who will advise you on planning permission, and help you to avoid making costly mistakes.

If a garage already exists on the property but is in a poor condition, improve its appearance by repairing and repainting the door, if possible.

Building a garage doesn't have to cost you an arm and a leg. Inexpensive alternatives include using a cement bag finish on the interior walls instead of plaster, and building the garage without a ceiling.

If possible, allow space for a workbench. Make sure you provide enough plug points for all your tools, as well as adequate overhead lighting.

Use the walls and rafters to store bicycles, garden equipment and furniture. Hang racks and shelves from the joists above, or simply put hooks into the beams to hang equipment. A spacious garage can even be used to store an extra freezer. However, don't let your garage become a dumping ground for all kinds of household junk.

Carport versus garage

Although some people feel that carports add no real value to a property, it is still much better than having nothing at all, and less expensive than building a garage. It is also not a permanent structure, which means you probably won't need permission to erect it. If all you need is undercover off-street parking, a carport will be the best solution. It can be paved or pebbled or simply filled with cement. Laying a grass lawn, however, is never a good idea.

Paving projects for your driveway

Paving the driveway in front of a garage or carport will add to the overall neatness of your property. There's a lot of preparatory work you can do before calling in the professional pavers.

Preparation

Make sure you choose a paving design that's cost-effective, structurally sound, and aesthetically pleasing. It should tie in with existing surfaces, and create a harmonious transition between the different levels.

Carefully survey and set out the area to be paved. Make sure that the surface is even and that there's adequate support for the paving. To prevent the area from becoming waterlogged, make sure it's properly drained, and that the soil in the area won't sag. To prevent movement after the paving has been completed, ensure that the soil isn't clay-like.

The construction phase

Start off by clearing the site. A well-prepared base, free of any materials that may later decompose, is absolutely essential. Lift existing paving and remove structures where new paving is required. Unless the base below it is sound, it's never a good idea to pave over existing paving.

Remove the earth so that the 'line and level' conform to the design criteria for the base of the paving. This will also ensure that there is an even distribution of materials, and allow you to better control the thickness of the layers.

Install a subsurface drainage system, and then install earth-retaining structures (to ensure an appealing and practical interface between the new paving and the higher or lower natural ground level). Earth-retaining structures are not the same as edge restraints, which, in the case of block or cobblestone paving, usually form part of the paving stage.

The road-layer works phase is the most important aspect of paving. The value of a solidly prepared base is not immediately apparent, and thus often the most neglected and skimped-on aspect of domestic paving works (and where some paving contractors might take shortcuts in order to present a bargain price). Clear up and cart away excess materials.

Our house: DRIVEWAY

The old cement pavers in the driveway were uneven and cracked. We knocked down the unsightly Vibacrete wall between the backyard and the drive way and moved the new brick wall, complete with picket fencing (a repeat of the new boundary wall), two metres forward, to add space to the new patio area. We tiled the driveway with dark grey stones. We also knocked down the outside stoep wall to allow direct access from the parking bay to the stoep. We erected wooden gates to tie in with the rest of the front area. We sealed the picket fencing and gates, and painted the walls the same colour as the rest of the exterior.

after

before

securing your home

The need for security has become an important fact of life. No homeowner can afford to leave a house unsecured and loved ones and possessions unprotected. From the basic burglar bar to armed response services, there are security options available to suit every pocket.

Although we might not like to admit it, security is a key concern for most South Africans. We all want the peace of mind to enjoy a restful night's sleep, or to go away on holiday knowing that our home is safe and not an easy target for criminals. The tricky part is in finding a way to provide your home with the best possible security, without making it feel as though you're living inside a maximum-security prison. And of course, in finding an alarm system that provides excellent security, but is not so complicated that even you can't operate it. Many a feud has started with the incessant howling of a neighbour's state-of-the-art (yet inoperable) alarm.

This chapter will provide you with some valuable and practical hints that will enable you to ensure that your home is a safe haven. It will provide you with available security options. In addition, there is an at-a-glance check list that will provide you with basic safety tips for your home.

Burglar bars and security doors

No secure home need look like a prison. Burglarproofing can be custom-made to suit your home, and comes in a wide variety of styles and colours. Choose a style that offers maximum protection, without detracting from the visual appeal of your home.

Security-door savvy

When buying a security door, make sure that both the frame of the security door and door frame to which you are going to attach it are strong and rigid. If they're not, the door won't be able to withstand much pressure, and will be of little use.

Security doors are made of steel, aluminum or wrought iron.

Make sure that the doors comply with industry standards, and, for your own protection, obtain a written guarantee for both the door and its installation.

Apart from fitting security doors on all outside doors, consider putting a security door at the entrance to your bedroom. This will ensure that, should an intruder gain access to your home, you will be safe, and able to alert police or your security company. Always keep your cellphone on your bedside table.

Style and security

Style and security? Yes, they can actually go hand-in-hand. Gone are the days when burglarproofing only made a house look ugly, unappealing, and more like a prison than a home. Custom-made burglar bars and burglarproofing that come in any shape, size and colour imaginable, allow you now to choose protection for your home that not only meets your security requirements, but also suits the style of your house. When you choose burglarproofing, make sure that it offers you both. There is such a wide variety of styles available, it is unlikely that you won't find burglarproofing that blends well with, and suits the style of your home. In fact, burglar bars can even be made to look older or to have a cottage pane appearance. So there really isn't any excuse for either not burglarproofing your home, or having burglar bars that stand out like a sore thumb, and detract from the visual appeal of your home.

Visit burglarproofing manufacturers' showrooms and look at the various designs and styles on offer. Decide which design or style will offer you maximum protection, and be best-suited to the style of your home. Your safest bet will be to have the burglarproofing professionally installed.

tip
If, for any reason, your burglar bars are secured with ordinary screws, put a spot of solder in each slot to prevent intruders unscrewing these from the outside.

Outside your house

Securing the perimeter of your home is just as important as securing the house itself. In fact, ideally, perimeter security should be such that intruders aren't able to gain access to your property in the first place, much less access to your home.

As convenient as it is for you to have direct access from your garage into your home, it is just as convenient for an intruder. Therefore, it's vitally important that you take the necessary measures to make your garage as secure as possible.

Keep the access door locked at all times and give each member of the household their own key. It may be an irritation today, but it could prevent a burglary tomorrow. If you have street-facing garage doors, make sure that they are locked at all times. Consider installing a motion-sensitive spotlight.

Garden safety

An overgrown garden not only looks shabby, but offers intruders a whole host of different hiding places. Make sure that your garden is free of any overgrown areas or corners covered with very dense growth. Also, make your garden as intruder unfriendly as possible! There's an immense variety of plants you can use that will not only look good in your garden, but will deter unlawful entry onto your property and into your home.

A thorny shrub, planted underneath a window sill, will deter an intruder from climbing through the window. Pyracantha and Berberis are good examples, but a scented rose will be even better. Cacti is ideal in very hot areas. Thorn trees, such as acacia, planted along a boundary wall, will deter any person from trying to climb over.

Do not, however, plant dense shrubbery that will offer hiding places to intruders. Dense rambling plants near the front reception and parking areas, or garage will only provide cover for anyone lying in wait for you to return home. Cacti, agave and cycads make a very attractive garden in these vulnerable areas.

If you insist on having shrubs, make sure they are low-growing and reach a maximum height of no more than half a metre. A creeper covering a carport is acceptable as well, as it provides shade, without providing much of a hiding place. Don't leave it unchecked, make sure you give it a regular trim.

If you decide to grow a hedge, use a mixture of plants and include prickly or thorny species. When you plant thorny shrubs or trees, place them in areas where intruders are most likely to try and gain access to your property. Plant prickly shrubs among other attractive plants.

Some of the Rubus species (e.g. blackberry and bramble) have long wavy shoots that twine among other plants, making it virtually impossible to climb through. Another option is the thorny *Carissa macrocarpa* or Natal plum. This very attractive indigenous species is also available as a groundcover, and is almost impenetrable. Its fragrant white flowers are followed by bright red fruit, attracting birds to your garden as well.

Ensure that none of your plants obscure any of the security lighting you have installed. Also, be sure to cut down any branches that hang invitingly over your boundary wall.

Shrubs planted directly around your house against your walls should not be too dense either. Plant only a few shrubs and make sure they are not too close to the windows. Or opt for a low-growing flowerbed instead. Rose bushes are perfect for beds directly beneath windows – they fill the air with a lovely fragrance and are very difficult to climb through.

In addition, consider using gravel chips in your garden as an extra safety measure. Use it as paving or even an alternative to grass; it also works well in between plants in flowerbeds. It will look good, save you the trouble of moving the lawn, keep weeds at bay AND is a sure-fire way of alerting you when someone approaches your house. Not a person in this world can walk softly on gravel!

Alarm systems and panic buttons

An alarm system that can be set at night while you're asleep inside the house, is ideal and will help ensure a peaceful night's rest. If your budget doesn't allow for motion detectors to be installed throughout the house, ask the security company to install them in key areas, such as a passage or central doorway. Make sure that there aren't any obstructions within the motion detectors' field of view.

Ensure that there are a number of panic buttons throughout the entire house. They should be easy to reach – place some at eye-level and others on ground level. Consider using a remote panic button as well. This you will be able to carry with you while working in the garden, for example, or while hanging out the washing.

In addition, you could consider installing perimeter beams in your garden. These will alert you of the presence of intruders well before they reach your house and try to gain access to it. An intercom system will allow you to regulate to whom you give permission to enter your property. In addition to all of these, you could also consider stoep enclosures, electric fencing, and installing remote-controlled gates for your driveway.

However, do be careful that you don't go completely overboard. You should never feel like a prisoner in your own home and security should never be such that the extent of it detracts from the visual appeal and value of your home.

Test your alarm every so often to make sure it is still in perfect working order, and that the security company arrives within an acceptable time. Don't test it on such a regular basis that it becomes a neighbourhood disturbance and an irritation.

Crime-fighting lighting

A well-lit property holds very little appeal to any would-be intruder. Proper lighting in all the right areas (i.e. adjacent to the street, and from which your property or house is most accessible), will deter any criminally inclined person from entering your property, because the risk of being seen and caught is too great.

Sensor lights, which automatically go on when movement is detected, are ideal for outdoor security lighting. They can be wired directly into your electrical system or installed by means of a plug. Although they are a little expensive, it is an investment well worth making. Sensor spotlights are ideal for the driveway or the entrance to your property, as well as the carport. If your budget allows, install sensor spotlights at the back and front door.

Photosensitive lights automatically come on when daylight dims to a certain level, which is especially useful when nobody is home. Alternatively, you can use timer switches that operate individual lights or appliances so it appears as though someone is home. Locate controls inside the house where they cannot be seen from the outside.

check list to protect your home

◄ Fit a security mortise deadlock to your main entry/exit door.

◄ Secure your garage, garden shed and any other outdoor buildings.

◄ Lock up ladders, lawnmowers, bikes and garden and electrical tools, anything that can be stolen, or used to gain access to your house.

◄ Don't hide door keys around the house or garden. Burglars know all the usual hiding spots and they are bound to find them.

◄ Secure skylights, garage doors and louvre doors so that they don't offer easy access to intruders.

◄ Check that all windows close properly.

◄ Make sure that none of the alarm sensors are obscured.

◄ Install smoke detectors throughout the house as an early fire warning.

◄ Make sure that outside areas are well lit at night and that there aren't any dark, overgrown corners where potential intruders can hide away to get

an idea of your movements and routines while they plan a break-in.

◄ Garages, free-standing or linked to the house, should be locked at all times – they often serve as tool storage areas and therefore contain all kinds of tools that can be used to break into your house.

◄ Consider investing in a guard dog, which will not only be a loyal friend but can also warn you in good time if there are intruders on your property.

Walls and fencing

Some architects will strongly advise you not to build boundary walls, and suggest that you create privacy by planting hedges. Or use plants, trees and flowers to create colourful border divisions between your property and the next. But in terms of security, these plantings will mean absolutely nothing and you can be sure that few insurance companies will agree with your architect's advice and suggestion.

Protect your house

Your first defence against intruders is your perimeter security, which would be high walls or fencing. Of course, a would-be intruder could easily scale the wall with a ladder, so don't rely solely on a high wall as your only defence.

A high wall, used in conjunction with security cameras or sensor lights, will be twice as effective in warding of intruders. Razor wire and barbed wire are equally effective to deter climbers, but do not look very attractive.

If you think razor or barbed wire looks too severe, there is a new similar type of wire on the market that has a much more attractive appearance and is designed to look like ivy.

Aptly called EINA-IVY, it is manufactured by Pretty Safe Security (it was developed in South Africa and has a worldwide patent), and comprises 4 mm galvanised razor-sharp fingers, twisted over a 1.5 m length of wire to look like branches and twigs.

The sharp spikes, simulating twigs, are fitted with synthetic leaves with a UV-stabilising polyester/nylon composition. These leaves are coated with a patented polyester/rubber composition designed to withstand harsh weather conditions, whether it be sunshine or strong winds.

If you want the best there is, and if your budget allows for it, have an electrified fence installed. Keep in mind, though, that while this may be practical for a fence on top of a high wall, it won't do to string an electrified fence around your front yard. Also, electrical fences are somewhat at the mercy of falling branches and birds, so keep this in mind before you make your final a decision. Make sure overhanging branches do not offer burglars an easy route over the fence.

Boundary options

If you do decide to build walls, and you can be sure your insurer will recommend this, there are a variety of options from which you can choose. Wall options range from simple stone and brick to concrete and timber. The style you choose will depend largely on your budget and naturally on the style of your house and the predominant function you wish the boundary to have, be it security or privacy.

If you'd like a fence, rather than a solid wall, there are also a number of options from which you can choose. From the traditional wooden, board and bamboo, to iron, aluminum and vinyl fences.

Aluminum fences are low-maintenance and you can achieve a classic look of iron with traditional pickets. There are also many decorative styles to choose from. Iron fences are strong and need the minimum maintenance.

Galvanised and aluminum-coated steel are resistant to rust, however, should the protective coating be scratched or come off, it could very well rust. Keep this in mind if you live in an area close to the sea where rust might be a problem. In which case it might be best to select pure aluminum fencing, because it won't rust.

Trellising can be constructed on walls and fencing that is vulnerable to intruders to increase the overall height of these boundaries and make entry more difficult.

Check with the authorities

Regulations and legislation regarding the kind of walls and fences you may build, or, in the case of electrical fences, what voltage is allowed, may apply in your municipal area. This is particularly true in private developments such as golfing estates, or sectional titles and any other security property developments.

You may find that the walls and fences you choose – even the type of burglar bars you are allowed to install – are regulated at many of these developments. Make sure you prescribe to the regulations and guidelines set out by the body corporate of such a development.

Establish where the building lines are on your property before you rush into building walls of any kind. You will need to get permission from your local authority or municipality to erect high walls, and you will also need approval if your new walls will encroach on any of the existing building lines.

In the case of new permanent structures, you will also need the go-ahead from your neighbours.

Even if it is not a 2-m wall and it is right at the back of your neighbours' properties it is still good neighbourly practice to inform them of your plans and building schedule.

Palisade fencing

Palisade fencing is very strong and durable, and can be made to look a little more attractive by planting greenery alongside the fence. Although it's a little expensive, it's worth every penny.

The bonus with this kind of fencing is that neither you nor your property will not be completely cut off from the outside world. You will still be able to see what's going on in the street and, for example, somebody from a security company driving past will be able to see if something is suspect on your property.

Palisade fencing should, ideally, be galvanised to ensure that it doesn't rust, and cost you even more. You can combine palisade fencing with walls, going for a one part wall and one part palisade fencing design. Palisade fencing looks good when it is done in the same style as the electronic gate.

Picket fences are traditional and homely looking, and there is a wide variety from which to choose. The pickets can be traditional, square or grand and formal. These fences work well with other traditional details such as trellises.

The most popular fencing materials include wood, chain-link, ornamental steel, ornamental aluminum, and vinyl. Wood is probably the most popular fencing material, because it is versatile, has a rustic charm and can be used in a variety of styles, making it look either very plain and simple, or more decorative when combined with lattices.

Opposite and below Your front gate creates one of the first impressions of your home and should reflect your personal style.

acknowledgements

Sponsor Addresses

A big thank you from the *Woman's Value* and ***dit*** makeover team to all our sponsors who made the *Woman's Value* and ***dit*** Dream Home project one of a kind.

Ackermans, (021) 555 1499

At home, (021) 914 8422

BPB GYPSUM t/a Lightweight Building Solutions, (011) 312 0920; www.bpbsa.com

Bosch Domestic Appliances, (011) 265 7800; www.bsh.co.za

Cape Gate, (011) 339 6001

ELFA Shelving and Basket Systems (021) 937 3177; www.cape-gate

Castor King, (021) 762 8610

Clicks, (011) 789 5760; www.clicks.co.za

Cobra Watertech (Pty) Limited, (011) 951 5000; www.cobrataps.co.za

Covenant Construction cc, civil engineering contractors, (021) 981 3329

Eagle Lighting, (021) 424 4071

Glas-it, (021) 424 3631

Henkel SA (Pty) Ltd, (011) 864 4950 and 0800 138 181; www.henkel.com

Ou Mutual, 0860 15 15 05; www.oldmutual.co.za

Owens Corning South Africa (Pty) Ltd, (011) 360 8200; www.thinkpinkaerolite.co.za

Van Dyck Carpets, (031) 912 1200 fax (031) 912 1220; www.vandyck.co.za

Mazista Tiles, (011) 462 4440; www.mazista.co.za

Pavatile, (021) 949 1986; www.pavatile.co.za

Plascon, 0860 20 40 60; www.plascon.co.za

The House of Woodoc, (046) 645 1109 and 0800 411 200; www.woodoc.com

Timbercity National franchise office, (012) 643 1181

Vaal Sanitaryware, (021) 555 0950

Van der Schyff Upholstery t/a Washiela Solomons Interiors, (021) 447 0704

Victorian Side, (021) 948 8250

Acknowledgements

A special thank you to the following people whose efficiency, fantastic service and generous sponsorship made our lives easy:

Salie Jacobs of GS Jacobs and Son Builders, for building and renovating the *Woman's Value* and ***dit*** Dream Home.

Daniel le Roux of Aspidistra Landscaping, for landscaping the water feature, patio and garden gravel and layout as well as the herb garden.

Country Rose, Stellenbosch, for supplying the rosemary and lavender bushes.

Marius Cloete of Pavatile, for sponsoring and supplying the pavers for the carpark.

Anthony Hubsch of Covenant Construction, civil engineering contractors, for paving the driveway.

Peter Osborn of At home, for sponsoring the kitchen-sink unit and spice rack.

Gerald Beeb, Bertha Hoffman and Liz Long of Vaal Sanitaryware, for sponsoring the bathroom basins.

Robin Smith of Eagle Lighting, for sponsoring the light fittings.

Marion Beamish, owner of Glas-it for supplying and fitting the window film.

Giuliana Errera from Italcotto for allowing us to shoot at their premises.

John Engels of Mazista, Paarden Eiland.

Robbie Webb of Cobra Watertech, Royal Cape Park, Ottery, Cape Town.

Natalie Vertue of BPB Gypsym, Epping Industria.

Inés McCarthy of Woodoc, Strand.

Nick Gosley of Timbercity, Woodstock.
Re-Faat Behardien of AMAC Services, and Zahir
Jacobs for collecting and returning all props.
Charlie Moir of Castor King for sponsoring
castors for the butcher's blocks in the kitchen.
The team at Weylandts, Greenpoint, for
organising furniture and props.

Thanks to Chris and Anne van Kaplan of
De Tafelberg Guesthouse, Molteno Road,
Oranjezicht, Cape Town, for letting us photo-
graph the renovations to their guesthouse for
this book.
And thanks to Marius Hitge, Ian de Kock, Allen
Leroux, Nicolas Whitehorn Landscaping (082 258
9293), Roma Kitchens and Euro Appliances
(Cape), Ital Cotto, Adriaan Oosthuizen, Terena le
Roux and Neville Lockhart for providing
locations for photographs.

Thank you to the following people for
providing information:
Mari Opperman, Colour consultant,
(082 371 9277)
Elsa Austin
Yvette Buitendag and Associates, architectural
designers and structural engineers,
(021) 852 8442
Peter Ludwig, branch manager of Pam Golding
Properties Southern Suburbs, Cape Town,
083 675 4094 and (021) 7975300
Pam Snyman of Pam Golding Training Academy
for Estate Agents, (021) 883 8533
The Nationlink Service Centre, (021) 975 9316
Berry Everitt, MD of the Chas Everitt
International property group
Coral Heath, national client service manager,
Pam Golding Properties,
(021) 797 5300

Ian Slot, chairman of Seeff Western Cape
Licensees
Tanya Swart of Old Mutual Personal Financial
Advice; call Old Mutual toll-free on
0860 151 505
Rob Johnson, executive director of Master
Builders & Allied Trades Association (MBA),
Western Cape, (021) 685 2625
Trellidor, (021) 790 3698
DM Geldenhuys
AD Dean, DistrictMail, Somerset West
Pretty Safe Security (Eina-Ivy), (021) 930 9300/1
and fax (021) 930 5384
Stephen Mills, horticulturist

Also a big thank you to the following
stores, shops and institutions for use of
their furniture, accessories and other items
as props for styling:
AA Paint, Mowbray, (021) 685 2123
Allison's Vintage Homestore, (021) 761 1405
Aspidistra Landscaping, 083 660 5552
At home, (021) 914 8422
Boardmans, (021) 671 7010
Bohemian Lifestyle, Long Street, Cape Town,
(021) 422 4462
Boeksentrum, (021) 406 3161
Bright House, (021) 683 6012
Congo Joe, Cavendish Square, (021) 671 2714
Country Rose, (021) 855 0755
Dash Décor, (021) 975 1821
Eagle Lighting, (021) 424 4071
Foschini @ home, (021) 670 3980
Game, Century City, (021) 555 7500
Goodwood Furniture Market,
(021) 592 3286
Hope Traditional Garden Furniture,
(021) 448 7485
Kenly, (021) 461 9140

L'Orangerie, (021) 761 8355
Nocturnal Affair, (021) 419 2291
Smiley's at home, (021) 762 2626
Tamarind Lifestyle, (021) 683 9656
The Plush Bazaar, (021) 419 8328
Weylandts Homestore, (021) 425 5282
Mad about house, 082 786 4232
Biggie Best, (021) 425 8315

To the photographers - Thanks guys for all
the long hours, the good 'eye' and creative
energy during our demanding four-month
renovating and shooting schedule.
Neville Lockhart
Anèl van der Merwe
Adriaan Oosthuizen
ASSISTANTS: Ronald James and Andries Joubert
STYLING AND PROPPING: Wilma Howells, Anneke
Blaise and Ilse de Klerk

DÉCOR MAKES: Tina Bester and Estee Laubscher
BUILDING OF SHELVING, STORAGE UNITS, AGEING OF GAR-
DEN POTS, LAYING OF PATIO AND BUILDING OF WATER FEA-
TURE: Salie Jacobs of GS Jacobs and Son Builders
(021) 637 4300 or 072 243 6943, Johan Crous,
and Daniel le Roux of Aspidistra Landscaping

index